Non-verbal Reasoning

Rebecca Brant

Name _____

Schofield & Sims

Introduction

Non-verbal reasoning skills enable you to solve problems that do not involve words. These skills are useful for school tests, such as the 11+. 'Non-verbal' means that no words are used, so in non-verbal reasoning tests, pictures are used instead of words. Non-verbal reasoning skills are important in other aspects of life too because you make many decisions based on what you see. By practising your non-verbal reasoning skills you will learn to look and think more carefully, using **logic**.

How to use this book

Before you start using this book, write your name in the box on the first page. Then decide how to begin. If you want a complete course on non-verbal reasoning, work right through the book. Another way to use the book is to dip into it when you want to find out about a particular type of question. The contents page or the index will help you to find the pages you need. Whichever way you choose, don't do too much at once – it's better to work in short bursts.

When you are ready to begin, find some scrap paper – or ask an adult for some. You may find this useful for your workings out. As you make a start, look out for these icons, which mark different parts of the text.

Explanation
This text explains key points about the question type and gives examples. Read it before you start the activities. Words shown like **this** appear in the combined index and glossary (page 96). The glossary focuses on terms used to explain reasoning questions. To understand maths terms, you may need to refer to maths books such as **Understanding Maths**.

Activities
These are the activities that you should complete. Most are multiple choice questions. Usually you show your answer by putting a circle round the letter that is below your chosen answer option. Occasionally you write your answer in the space provided. **After you have worked through all the activities on a page, turn to pages 70 to 94 to check your answers. These pages explain how each correct answer is reached. Read them carefully.** When you are sure that you understand a question type, tick the box beside it on the Contents page.

Hint
This text gives you extra information on how you might tackle a particular activity.

Important
This text tells you something that you must remember if you want your answers to be correct.

Do and learn
This text describes a practical activity that will help you to understand a particular question type.

Contents

Tick the box when you have worked through the topic.

Similarities and differences — 4

☐ Similarities — 4
☐ Similarities practice pages — 7
☐ Odd one out — 11
☐ Odd one out practice pages — 13
☐ Analogies — 17
☐ Analogies practice pages — 20

Missing and hidden shapes — 24

☐ Series — 24
☐ Series practice pages — 27
☐ Hidden shapes — 31
☐ Hidden shapes practice pages — 33
☐ Matrices — 37
☐ Matrices practice pages — 40
☐ Reflected shapes — 44
☐ Reflected shapes practice pages — 47

Cubes, codes and combinations — 51

☐ Nets of cubes — 51
☐ Nets of cubes practice pages — 54
☐ Codes — 58
☐ Codes practice pages — 60
☐ Combined shapes — 64
☐ Combined shapes practice pages — 66

Answers — 70

Test and revision tips — 95

Index and glossary — 96

Similarities

In **similarity** questions, you look at a set of pictures. You work out what features they have that are the same. You then choose another picture that shares all those features. This makes the picture **similar** to the others.

Finding common features

Pictures with features 'in common'
(this means that they all have some of the same features)

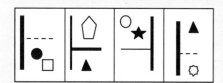

These pictures look different. But if you look carefully you will find features that all four pictures have in common.

Hint Ignore any **differences** between the pictures. Focus on similarities.

Common features
Each picture contains:
a) Two lines, each of different thickness.
b) Lines that are **perpendicular** (at right angles to each other) but do not cross.
c) Two different shapes – one white and one black.

 Make a list of the common features shared by the four pictures below.

Pictures with features in common

Common features

1.

a) <u>each contains a white rectangle</u>

b) _____

c) _____

2.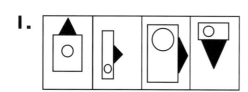

a) _____

b) _____

c) _____

d) _____

Similarities

Choosing a similar picture

After you have found all the common features, you need to find another picture that shares all these features.

Here are the pictures from the top of page 4, plus five answer pictures. You have to choose one answer picture that is similar to the other four. Look back at the **Common features** list. Which answer picture has all these features?

Pictures with features in common

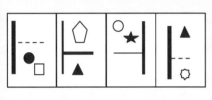 Use the notes below to help you.

Answer pictures

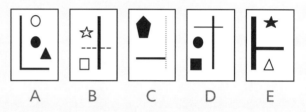

Hint Decide which pictures are **not** similar before looking for the one that **is**.

a) Two lines, each of different thickness.

b) Perpendicular lines that do not cross.

c) One white shape and one black.

Answer: E

The lines in **A** are the same thickness, so it can't be **A**.

All the pictures have perpendicular lines, but the lines in **B** and **D** cross. So neither **B** nor **D** is the picture you are looking for.

That leaves you with pictures **C** and **E**. **C** only has one shape, so it can't be **C**. That leaves you with **E**, which has two different shapes, one black and one white.

 Look back to questions 1 and 2 on page 4. Look at each common feature. See which of the pictures below share this feature. Circle the letters. When you find a picture that shares all the features, you can write the answer.

Answer pictures

1.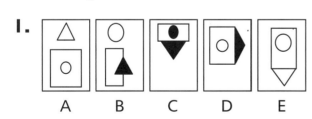

Common features

a) A   B   C   D   E

b) A   B   C   D   E

c) A   B   C   D   E

Answer: ___

2.

a) A   B   C   D   E

b) A   B   C   D   E

c) A   B   C   D   E

d) A   B   C   D   E

Answer: ___

Similarities

Here are four more pictures with features **in common** plus five answer pictures. The common features of the pictures on the left are listed below.

1. Pictures with features in common

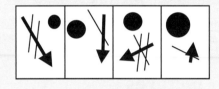

Answer pictures

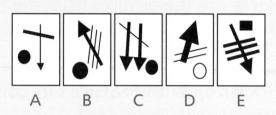

A   B   C   D   E

Common features

a) A single black arrow that is the same thickness in each picture.

b) At least one thin black line. These lines are the same thickness in each picture.

c) An arrow crossing another line.

d) A black circle.

Look at each common feature above. See which of the pictures on the right share this feature. Circle the letters. When you find a picture that shares all the features, you can write the answer.

a) A   B   C   D   E

b) A   B   C   D   E

c) A   B   C   D   E

d) A   B   C   D   E   **Answer:** ___

2. Now try this one. Start by listing the common features, ignoring the **differences**. Then circle the letters to find the answer.

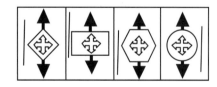

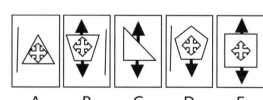

A   B   C   D   E

Common features

a) _____

b) _____

c) _____

a) A   B   C   D   E

b) A   B   C   D   E

c) A   B   C   D   E

Answer: ___

Now try some more **similarities** questions. Which picture on the right belongs to the group on the left? Circle the letter. If you get stuck, go back to pages 4 to 6 for some reminders.

Pictures with features in common

Answer pictures

1.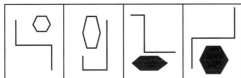

   A   B   C   D   E

2.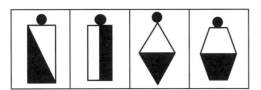

   A   B   C   D   E

3.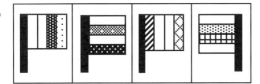

   A   B   C   D   E

4.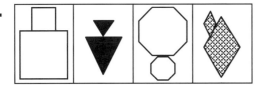

   A   B   C   D   E

5.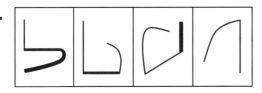

   A   B   C   D   E

6.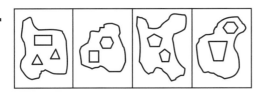

   A   B   C   D   E

Which picture on the right belongs to the group on the left? Circle the letter.

**Pictures with features
in common**

Answer pictures

1.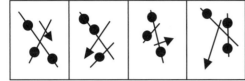

    A   B   C   D   E

2.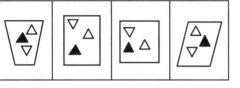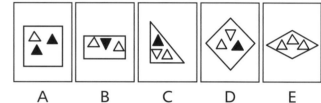

    A   B   C   D   E

3.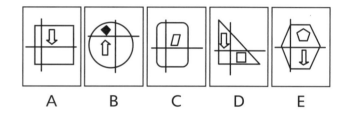

    A   B   C   D   E

4.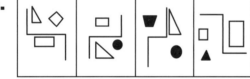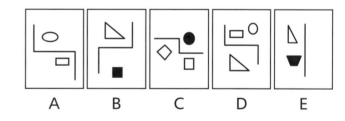

    A   B   C   D   E

5.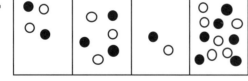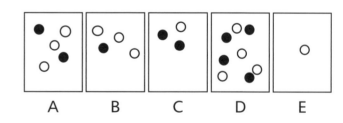

    A   B   C   D   E

6.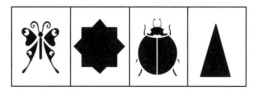

    A   B   C   D   E

Which picture on the right belongs to the group on the left? Circle the letter.

Pictures with features in common

Answer pictures

1.
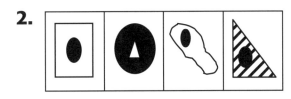

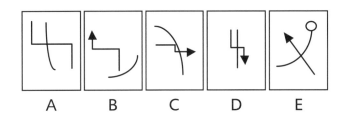

A   B   C   D   E

2.
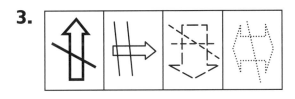

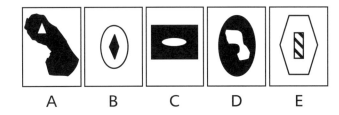

A   B   C   D   E

3.
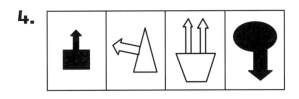

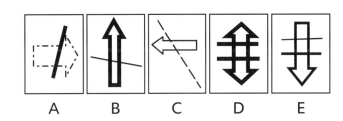

A   B   C   D   E

4.
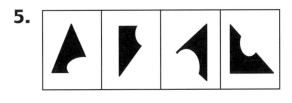

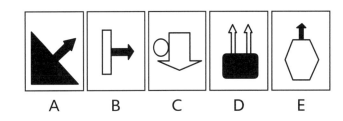

A   B   C   D   E

5.
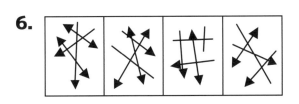

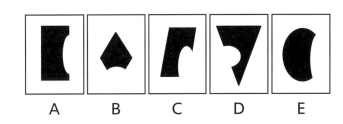

A   B   C   D   E

6.

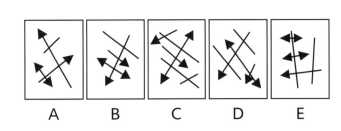

A   B   C   D   E

Which picture on the right belongs to the group on the left? Circle the letter.

**Pictures with features
in common**

Answer pictures

1.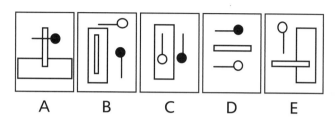

2.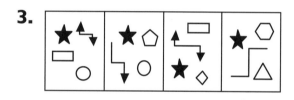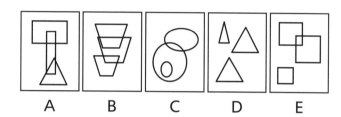

3.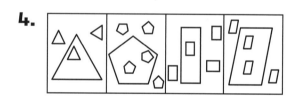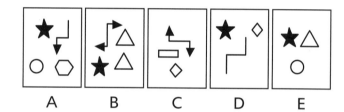

4.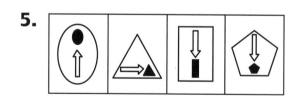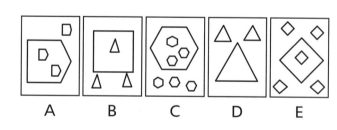

5.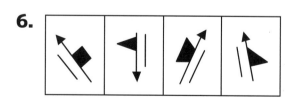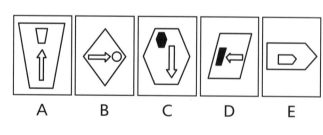

6.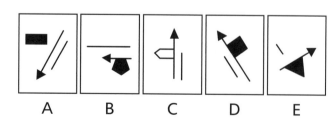

Odd one out questions are the opposite to **similarities** questions. Rather than looking for the one picture that is similar to all the others, you look for the one picture that is different – the odd one out.

Finding common features

First you need to find out what four of the pictures have **in common**. You can then find the **one** picture that does **not** have this feature.

For example:

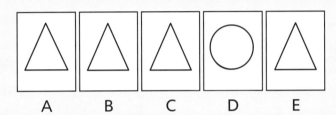

Four of the pictures are triangles and only one is a circle. **D** is therefore the odd one out.

Answer: <u>D</u>

Find the odd one out in the following groups. Circle the correct letter.

1.

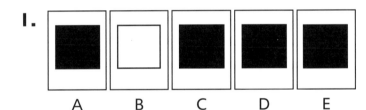

2.

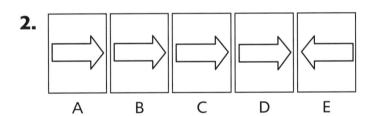

The above examples have only one feature that is different. The pictures below have a few **differences**. You have to ignore the differences and find the **one** thing that four of them have **in common**.

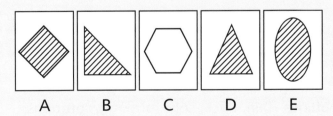

Four of the pictures are striped and only **C** is white. **C** is the odd one out.

Answer: <u>C</u>

Odd one out

 Write down next to the pictures the **one** thing that four of them have **in common**. Ignore any **differences**.

1.

A   B   C   D   E

_____
_____

2.

A   B   C   D   E

_____
_____

> **!** Some **odd one out** pictures have lots of differences. You must remember to look only for the similarities.

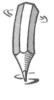 The following pictures have lots of differences. There is one **similarity** that is **common to** four of the pictures. Write the similarity on the line. Then circle the letter to show the odd one out.

3.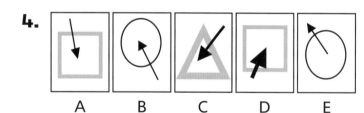

A   B   C   D   E

_____
_____

4.

A   B   C   D   E

_____
_____

5.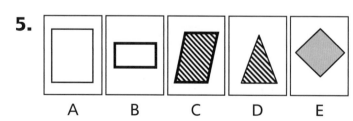

A   B   C   D   E

_____
_____

> **Hint** In **odd one out** pictures, look out for similarities relating to shape, patterns and shading, direction of arrows, straight and curved lines or sides, number of sides, shapes and lines, style of lines and outlines (thin, thick, solid, broken), rotations, symmetry and lines that cross or do not.

Which picture is the odd one out? Circle the letter. If you get stuck, go back to pages 11 and 12 for some reminders.

1.

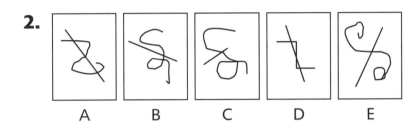

A   B   C   D   E

2.

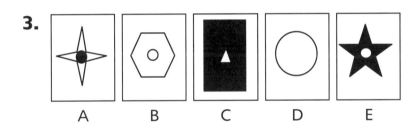

A   B   C   D   E

3.

A   B   C   D   E

4.

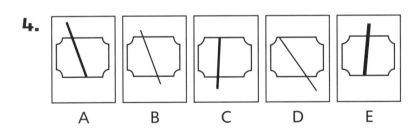

A   B   C   D   E

5.

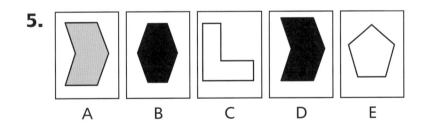

A   B   C   D   E

6.

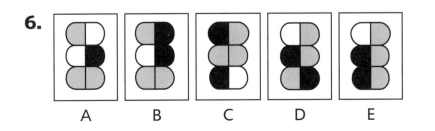

A   B   C   D   E

Which picture is the **odd one out**? Circle the letter.

1.

| A | B | C | D | E |

2.

| A | B | C | D | E |

3.

| A | B | C | D | E |

4.

| A | B | C | D | E |

5.

| A | B | C | D | E |

6.

| A | B | C | D | E |

Which picture is the odd one out? Circle the letter.

1.

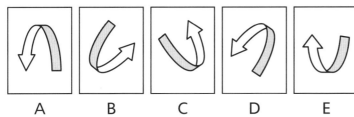

A B C D E

2.

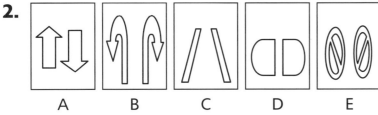

A B C D E

3.

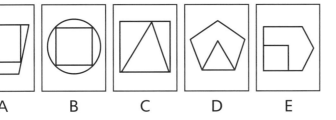

A B C D E

4.

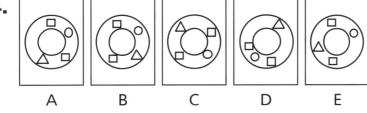

A B C D E

5.

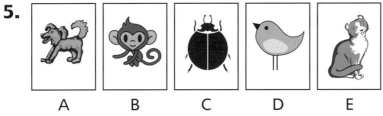

A B C D E

6.

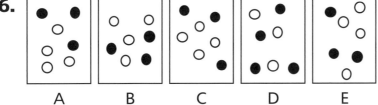

A B C D E

Which picture is the **odd one out**? Circle the letter.

1.

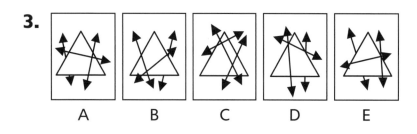

A   B   C   D   E

2.

A   B   C   D   E

3.

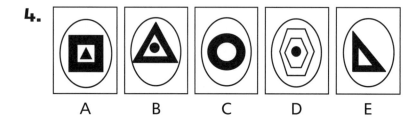

A   B   C   D   E

4.

A   B   C   D   E

5.

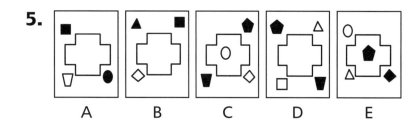

A   B   C   D   E

6.

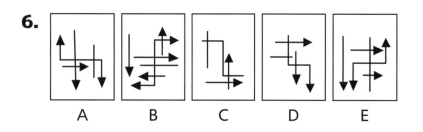

A   B   C   D   E

Analogies

An **analogy** is a comparison of similar things. In non-verbal reasoning analogy questions, you look for ways in which two pictures go together. You look at the first pair of pictures and find the **similarities** and **differences**. Then you identify another pair where the two pictures relate to each other in a similar way. You do this by choosing the final picture of that second pair.

Simple changes

For example: Have a look at these two pictures.

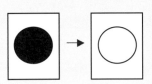

The first picture is a **black circle** and the second is a **white circle**. The link between the two pictures is that the **shape** has stayed the **same** but the **colour** has **changed** from black to white.

The next picture, below, is a black triangle. To find its pair you need to link it in the same way as the two shapes above are linked. So you need to keep the shape the same but change the colour from black to white.

Answer pictures

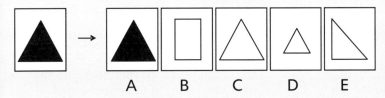

A   B   C   D   E

The black equilateral triangle links with the white equilateral triangle of the same size. The connection between the two triangles is the same as the connection between the two circles at the top of the page.

Answer: C

Write down the similarities and differences that link the two pictures.

1.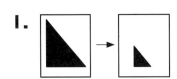

a) _____

b) _____

2.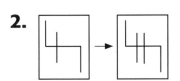

a) _____

b) _____

At the foot of page 17, in questions 1 and 2, you worked out the links between pictures. Apply those links to a second pair of pictures for each. Choose the picture that goes with the third picture below. Circle the letter.

Pictures with features in common   Answer pictures

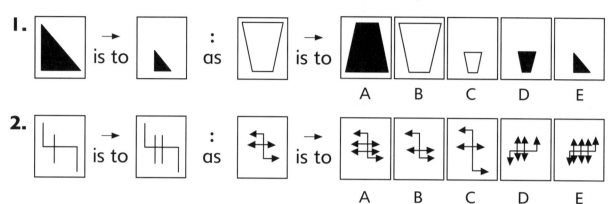

Rotations

Sometimes you need to decide whether the object in a picture has been **rotated** (spun around). Imagine that the object is pinned to the paper and one end of it is moved round. Each time it moves through a **right angle**, it moves 90°. It may move **clockwise** or **anticlockwise**.

In the first three diagrams below, the blue dot helps you to see the rotation.

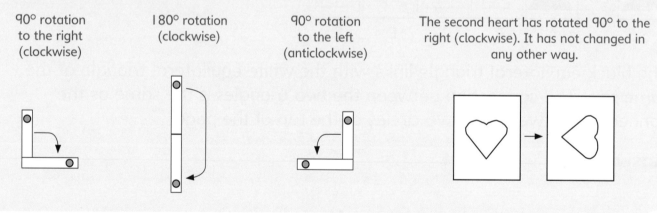

90° rotation to the right (clockwise)

180° rotation (clockwise)

90° rotation to the left (anticlockwise)

The second heart has rotated 90° to the right (clockwise). It has not changed in any other way.

Compare the two objects. Describe how the second one has been rotated.

3.

_____

4.

_____

Analogies

Change in colour or size

Sometimes the first and second objects may be different colours or sizes as well as having been rotated.

 Which of the five shapes goes with the third one to make a pair like the two on the left? Circle the letter.

1. is to : as is to

                                                   A   B   C   D   E

Reflections

When an object has been **reflected** you need to imagine that a mirror has been placed next to it. You will see a back-to-front **image** of the object. This is a reflection. When answering your first few reflection questions, use a real mirror to see the reflected shape. But do not depend on it for too long.

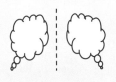

mirror line

The thought bubble on the left has been reflected in the **vertical** (↕) mirror line to create the reflected thought bubble on the right.

-------- mirror line

The thought bubble on the left has been reflected in a **horizontal** (↔) mirror line.

Hint   Look at where parts of the picture are in relation to the mirror line. If they are close to it, they will also be close to it in the reflection.

 Decide which of the five shapes goes with the third one to make a pair like the two on the left. Circle the letter.

!   Whatever links the first pair of pictures must also link the second pair. If the first pair of pictures uses a horizontal mirror line, the second pair must do the same.

2.   : →

                                                    A   B   C   D   E

Which of the five shapes goes with the third one to make a pair like the two on the left? Circle the letter. If you get stuck, go back to pages 17 to 19 for some reminders.

1.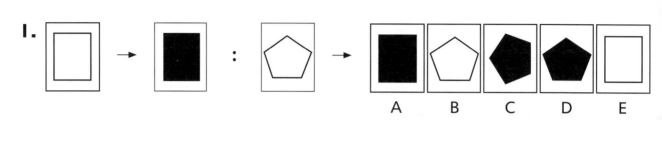

2.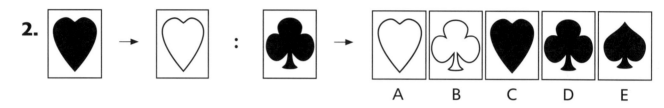

3.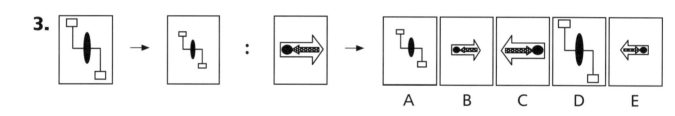

4.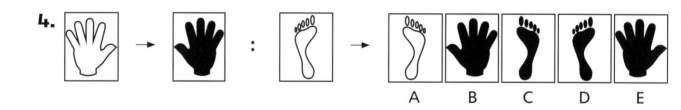

5.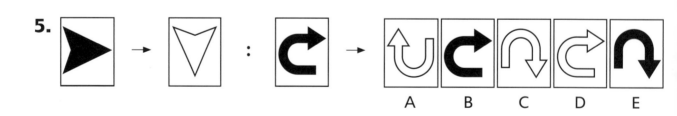

6.

Which of the five shapes goes with the third one to make a pair like the two on the left? Circle the letter.

1.

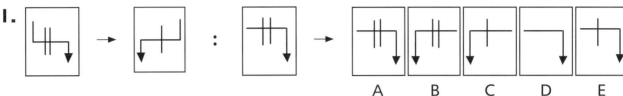

2.

3.

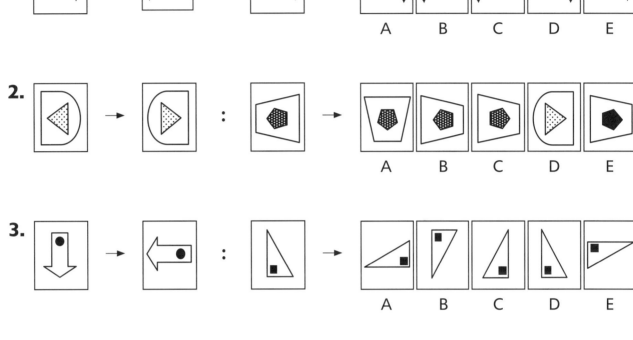

4.

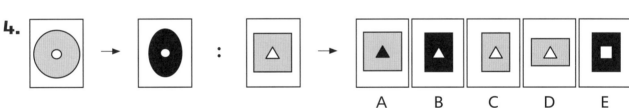

5.

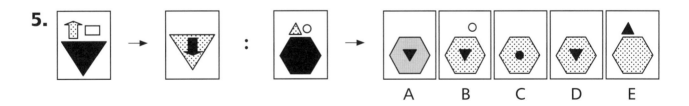

6.

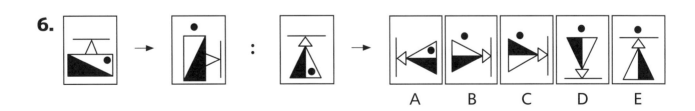

Which of the five shapes goes with the third one to make a pair like the two on the left? Circle the letter.

1.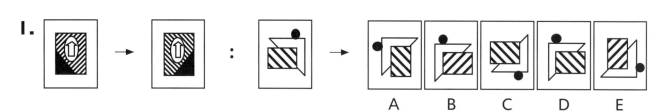

      A   B   C   D   E

2.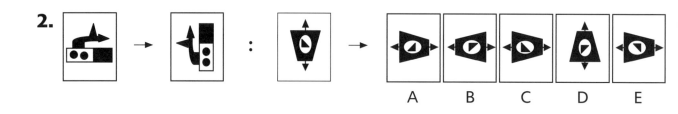

      A   B   C   D   E

3.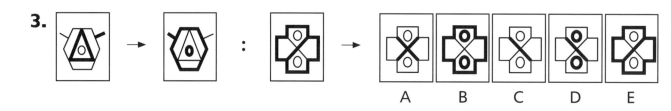

      A   B   C   D   E

4.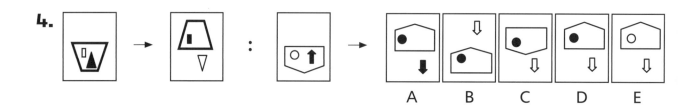

      A   B   C   D   E

5.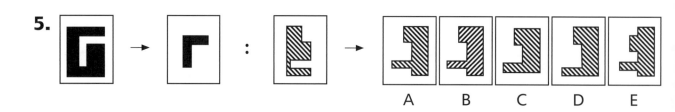

      A   B   C   D   E

6.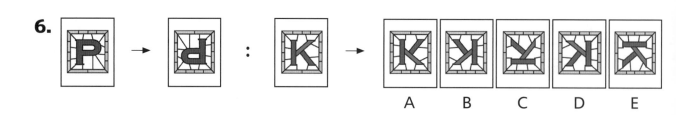

      A   B   C   D   E

Which of the five shapes goes with the third one to make a pair like the two on the left? Circle the letter.

1.

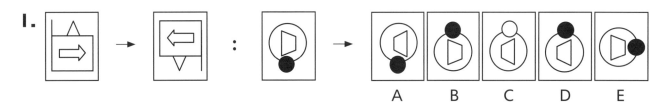

2.

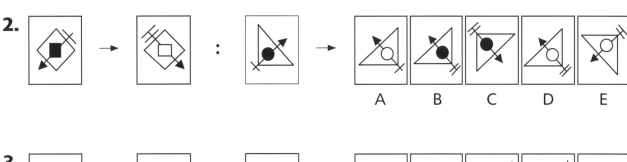

3.

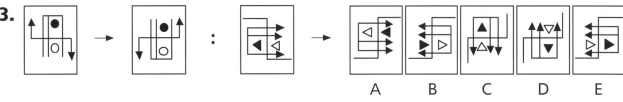

4.

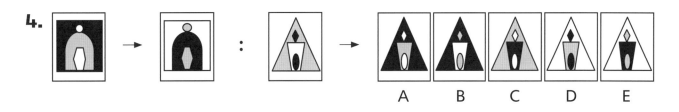

5.

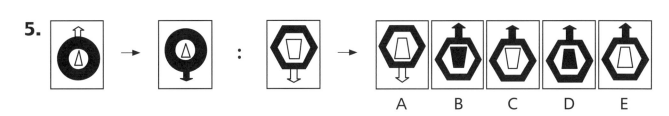

6.

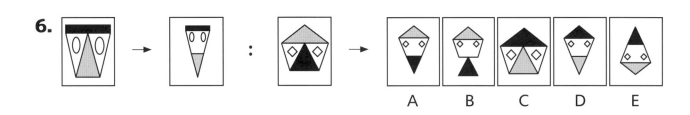

In **series** or **sequence** questions, you look at a set of pictures that are arranged in order. You need to find out the rule or rules linking the pictures, so that you can work out which picture comes next. There are two types of pattern.

The repeating pattern

You need to work out how the pattern is being repeated.

For example: The pattern A Z A Z A Z A Z is simply two letters repeated one after the other. When three letters are used the pattern becomes slightly more difficult: A B C A B C A B C. The letters are repeated in the same order and are used more than once.

Look at this sequence.

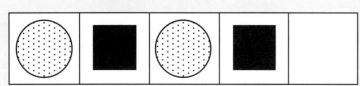

The pattern here is spotty circle, black square, spotty circle, black square. So what comes next?

Look at the five pictures below. Which one would continue the pattern above?

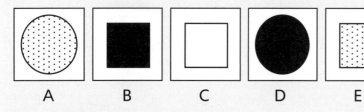

The pattern is circle, square, circle, square, so the next picture is a circle. The circle needs to be a spotty one, so the answer must be **A**. Picture **A** should take the place of the empty box above.

Answer: A

Look at the four pictures. Write on the lines on the right a description of the repeating pattern. Then draw in the empty box a picture of what would come next.

1.

_____

_____

2.

_____

_____

Which one of the five squares on the right should take the place of the empty box? Circle the letter.

1.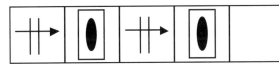

                                          A   B   C   D   E

2.   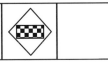

                                          A   B   C   D   E

The non-repeating pattern

In this series of pictures, each object is slightly different. They follow a pattern. Work out how the pictures change.

> **Hint**   Look at the colours, shapes, numbers of objects and their direction. Ask, **What stays the same? What changes?**

What stays the same in each picture?
Each has a black **diagonal** line from top left to bottom right. Each has a circle on the right-hand side of the line.

What changes in each picture?
The circle gets darker as it goes from left to right. The position of the circle changes. It moves down the line.

Now look at the five pictures below. One of them completes the pattern above. If it is placed in the empty box, the pattern will be continuous.

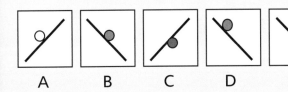

A   B   C   D   E

You are looking for a line from top left to bottom right. Ignore **A** and **C** because the lines run in the wrong direction.

The circle should get darker each time. Ignore **E** because it is the same colour as the last picture in the series.

That leaves **B** and **D**. Both have the correct type of line, with the circle on the right-hand side. They are both the correct colour (between the colours of the second and fourth pictures of the series).

Look at the position of the circle, which gradually moves down the line. The missing picture should show the circle halfway down the line.

The answer is **B**.

Answer: <u>B</u>

Series

Look at the **series** of pictures. Make a list of all the **similarities** and **differences**. Then choose the picture that completes the series.

 Hint) Decide which pictures are **not** possible before looking for the one that **is**.

1.

Similarities

_____

_____

_____

Differences

_____

_____

_____

Now choose the picture that would complete the series. Circle the letter.

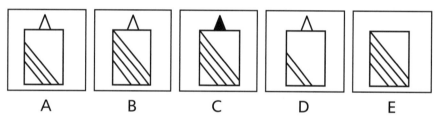

2.

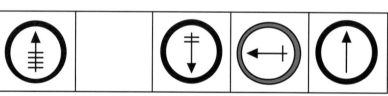

Similarities

_____

_____

_____

Differences

_____

_____

_____

Now choose the picture that would complete the series. Circle the letter.

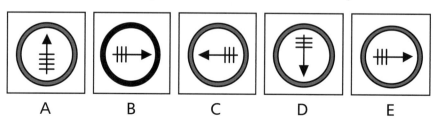

Which picture on the right belongs to the group on the left? Circle the letter. If you get stuck, go back to pages 24 to 26 for some reminders.

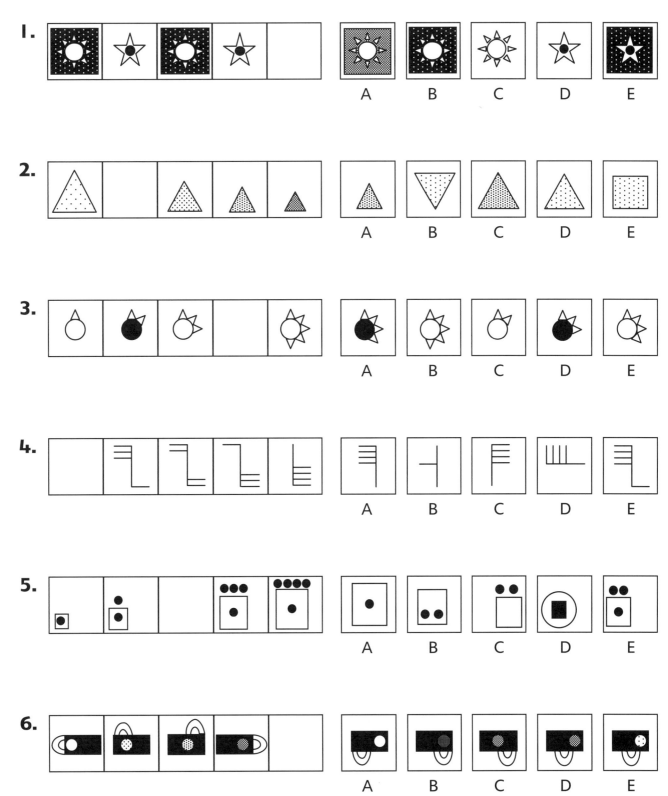

Which picture on the right belongs to the group on the left? Circle the letter.

1.

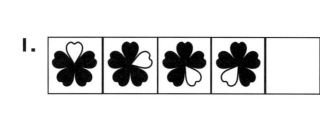 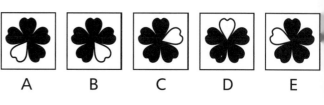

A   B   C   D   E

2.

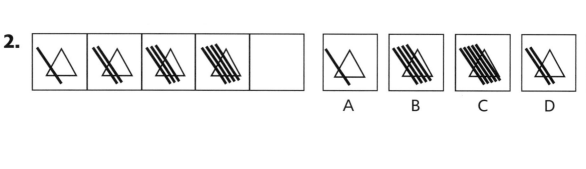

A   B   C   D   E

3.

A   B   C   D   E

4.

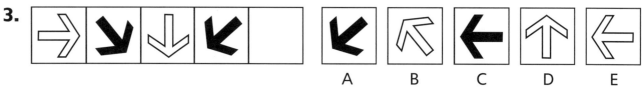

A   B   C   D   E

5.

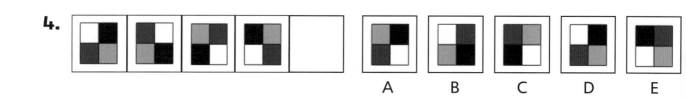

A   B   C   D   E

6.

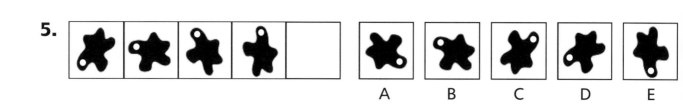

A   B   C   D   E

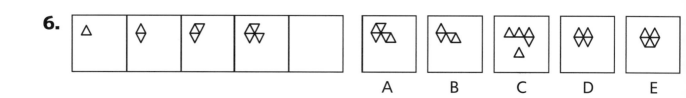

Series practice page 3

Which picture on the right belongs to the group on the left? Circle the letter.

1.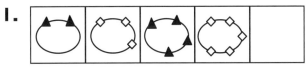

A   B   C   D   E

2.

A   B   C   D   E

3.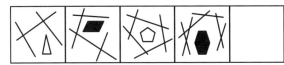

A   B   C   D   E

4.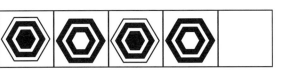

A   B   C   D   E

5.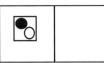

A   B   C   D   E

6.

A   B   C   D   E

Which picture on the right belongs to the group on the left? Circle the letter.

1.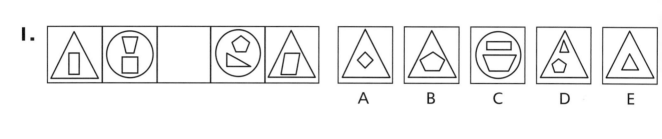

2.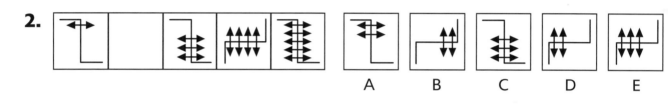

3.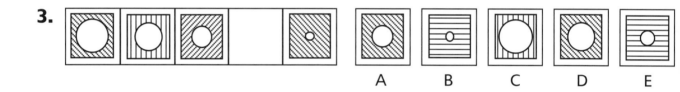

4.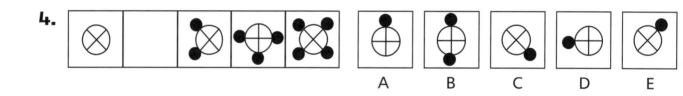

5.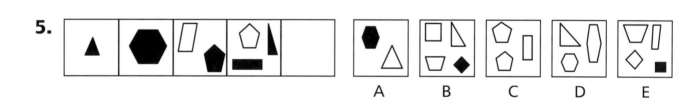

6.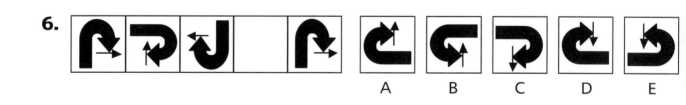

Hidden shapes

In **hidden** shapes questions you look at a set of pictures in order to find a smaller shape hidden within one of them. In many of the other types of non-verbal reasoning question, you need to look for rules, **similarities** or **differences**. This is **not** the case with hidden shape questions.

Simple shapes

In which larger shape is the smaller shape on the left hidden?

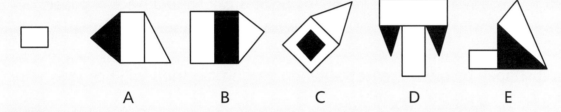

A   B   C   D   E

> ! Always look very carefully at the small shape on the left.

The shape on the left is a small rectangle (a four-sided shape with four **right angles**). Now look at each of the larger shapes in turn and see whether the small white rectangle is hidden within it.

A has a white rectangle within it, but it is much bigger than the one you are looking for.
B also has a white rectangle, but once again, it is too big.
C does not have any rectangles in it, only squares and a triangle.
D is made up of two white rectangles, but yet again they are too big.
E has a small white rectangle within it that is exactly the right size. (The rectangle is shown in blue below.) So **E** is the answer.

Small rectangle

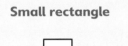

Small rectangle within larger shape

Answer: <u>E</u>

1. In which larger shape is the smaller shape on the left hidden?

Look carefully at the smaller shape. It is a white right-angled triangle. When you have found the answer, circle the letter.

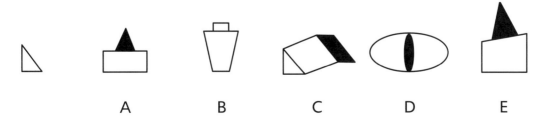

A   B   C   D   E

Hidden shapes

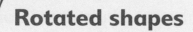

![book icon] **Rotated shapes**

In more difficult **hidden** shape questions, the smaller shapes are **rotated**. You did some work on rotations in the **Analogies** section (page 18). So you will know that all the objects below are the same shape. They have just been rotated in different ways.

> **!** When a shape is rotated it is **not** flipped over. It simply spins around as if one point is pinned to a piece of paper.

The small shapes below are rotated when hidden. So they will not look exactly the same as they do on the left.

In which larger shape is the smaller shape on the left hidden? Circle the letter.

1.

     A   B   C   D   E

2.

     A   B   C   D   E

![book icon] **Complex shapes**

If the small shape is more complex, break it up into smaller pieces.

For example: Think of a shape like this as a line with a small square on each end. This gives you more to look for in the bigger pictures.

In which larger shape is the smaller shape on the left hidden? Circle the letter.

3.

     A   B   C   D   E

4.

     A   B   C   D   E

In which larger shape on the right is the smaller shape on the left hidden? Circle the letter. If you get stuck, go back to pages 31 and 32 for some reminders.

1.

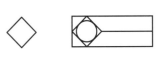

A   B   C   D   E

2.

A   B   C   D   E

3.

A   B   C   D   E

4.

A   B   C   D   E

5.

A   B   C   D   E

6.

            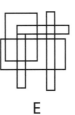

A   B   C   D   E

In which larger shape on the right is the smaller shape on the left **hidden**? Circle the letter.

1.

A   B   C   D   E

2.

 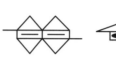

A   B   C   D   E

3.

A   B   C   D   E

4.

A   B   C   D   E

5.

A   B   C   D   E

6.

A   B   C   D   E

In which larger shape on the right is the smaller shape on the left hidden? Circle the letter.

1.

              A   B   C   D   E

2.

              A   B   C   D   E

3.

              A   B   C   D   E

4.

              A   B   C   D   E

5.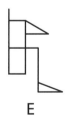

              A   B   C   D   E

6.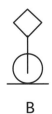

              A   B   C   D   E

In which larger shape on the right is the smaller shape on the left **hidden**?
Circle the letter.

1.

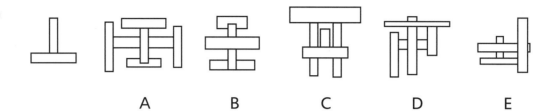

A   B   C   D   E

2.

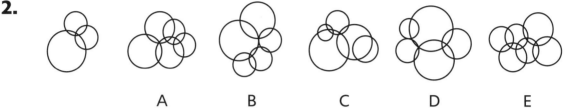

A   B   C   D   E

3.

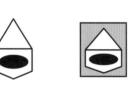   

A   B   C   D   E

4.

A   B   C   D   E

5.

 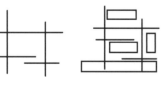   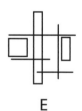

A   B   C   D   E

6.

A   B   C   D   E

Matrices

A **matrix** (plural **matrices**) is a grid made up of four or nine squares. You look at each square to find a pattern. This will help you to work out what the missing picture is. There are three main types of pattern.

Sequences

Use the same rules that you used in the **Series** section (pages 24 to 26) for working out **series** or **sequence** matrices. First find the pattern by looking at each **row** (↔) and then each **column** (↕). You need to look at both to check that you have correctly identified the pattern. Focus on the object within each square. Once you have worked out the pattern, choose the picture to fill the gap.

For example:

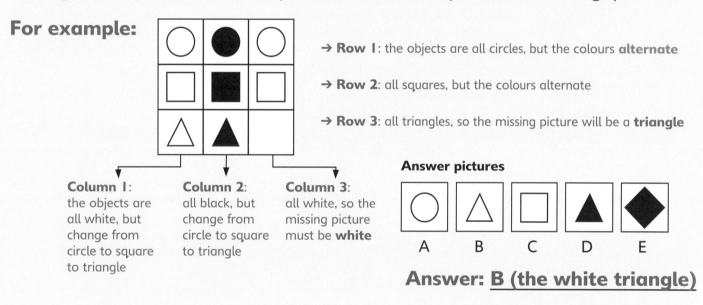

→ **Row 1**: the objects are all circles, but the colours **alternate**

→ **Row 2**: all squares, but the colours alternate

→ **Row 3**: all triangles, so the missing picture will be a **triangle**

Column 1: the objects are all white, but change from circle to square to triangle

Column 2: all black, but change from circle to square to triangle

Column 3: all white, so the missing picture must be **white**

Answer pictures

A B C D E

Answer: <u>B (the white triangle)</u>

Look at the matrix below. Find the pattern for each row and column and write it on the lines provided. Then choose the answer picture that completes the matrix. Circle the letter.

1.

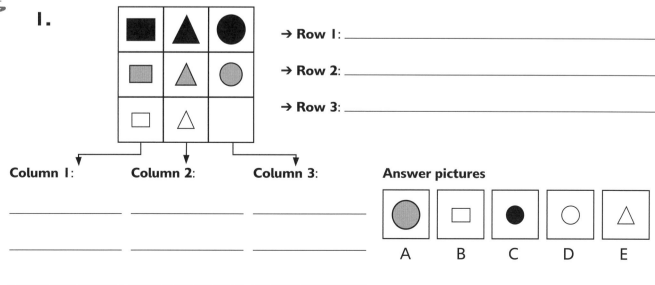

→ **Row 1**: _____

→ **Row 2**: _____

→ **Row 3**: _____

Column 1: _____ **Column 2:** _____ **Column 3:** _____

_____ _____ _____

_____ _____ _____

_____ _____ _____

Answer pictures

A B C D E

Matrices

Reflections

In these **matrices** you need to recognise when a shape has been **reflected**. The lines crossing the grids are the mirror lines.

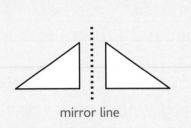

mirror line

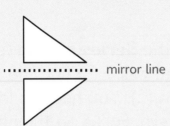

mirror line

Hint Look to see whether parts of the picture always point to a certain part of the grid.

For example:

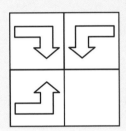

This matrix does not follow a pattern or **sequence**. Each picture is an arrow and all the arrows point in different directions. However, all the arrow heads face towards the centre. This is because they are all reflections of each other. Place a mirror along the grid lines and you will see.

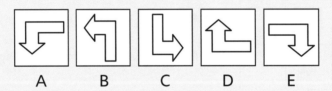

A   B   C   D   E

To find the missing picture you need to work out what the reflection would look like.

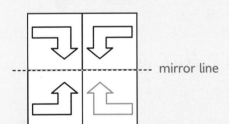

mirror line

Answer: <u>D</u>

Which is the missing picture? Use a mirror to help you. Circle the letter.

1.

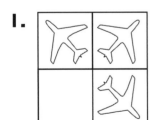

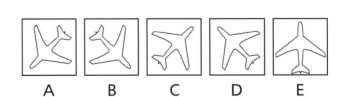

A   B   C   D   E

2.

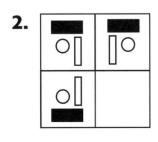

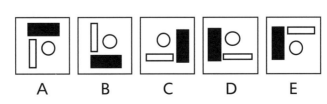

A   B   C   D   E

Rotations

In these matrices the shapes have been **rotated**. Rotations and reflections can look very similar but you should be able to see the **difference**. Look carefully at the penguin's beak.

This picture has been rotated. The penguin is looking over his right shoulder in both pictures. The picture has just been spun around.

point of rotation

This picture has been reflected. The penguin is looking over his right shoulder in the first picture and his left shoulder in the second. It's as though the picture has been flipped over.

Hint To find a rotation, imagine a pin stuck in the centre of the grid, and the pictures spinning round it. Spin the book around if it helps.

For example: In this **matrix**, the penguin rotates 90° **clockwise** from top left to top right. Imagine spinning him round another 90° to take his place in the empty square. What would he look like? Where would his beak be?

As the penguin rotates, his head always faces the outside corner of the grid, so it can't be **A** or **B**. **C**, **D** and **E** are all pointing in the right direction but **D** is identical to the bottom left square so this can't be the right choice as the penguin must move each time. In **C** and **E** the beaks are on different sides. The penguin should have his beak over his right shoulder so **C** is the correct answer.

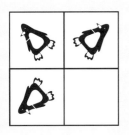

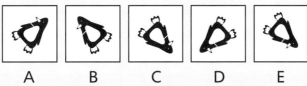

A   B   C   D   E

Answer: C

Which of the five pictures on the right should fill the empty square? Circle the letter.

1.

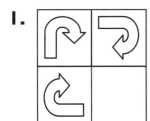

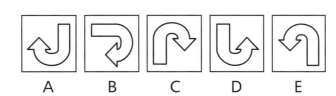

A   B   C   D   E

2.

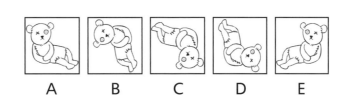

A   B   C   D   E

Which picture on the right best fits into the space in the grid on the left?
Circle the letter. If you get stuck, go back to pages 37 to 39 for some reminders.

1.

A   B   C   D   E

2.

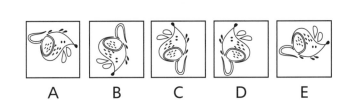

A   B   C   D   E

3.

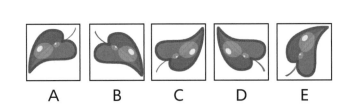

A   B   C   D   E

4.

A   B   C   D   E

5.

A   B   C   D   E

6.

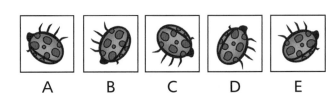

A   B   C   D   E

Which picture on the right best fits into the space in the grid on the left? Circle the letter.

1.

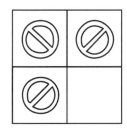

A   B   C   D   E

2.

A   B   C   D   E

3.

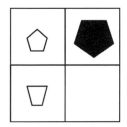

A   B   C   D   E

4.

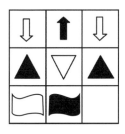

A   B   C   D   E

5.

A   B   C   D   E

6.

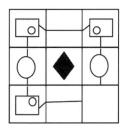

A   B   C   D   E

Which picture on the right best fits into the space in the grid on the left? Circle the letter.

1.

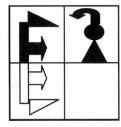

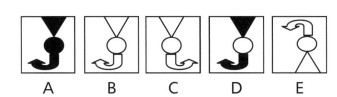

A   B   C   D   E

2.

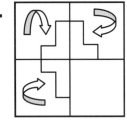

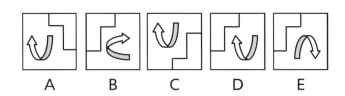

A   B   C   D   E

3.

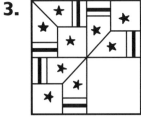

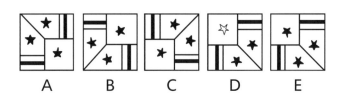

A   B   C   D   E

4.

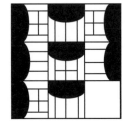

A   B   C   D   E

5.

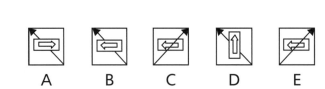

A   B   C   D   E

6.

A   B   C   D   E

Which picture on the right best fits into the space in the grid on the left? Circle the letter.

1.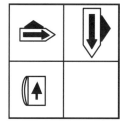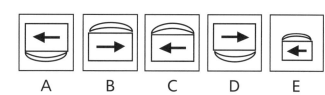

A   B   C   D   E

2.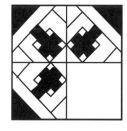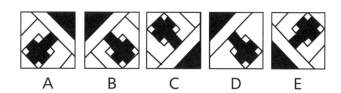

A   B   C   D   E

3.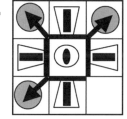

A   B   C   D   E

4.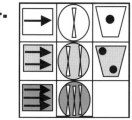

A   B   C   D   E

5.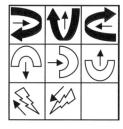

A   B   C   D   E

6.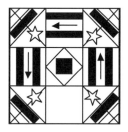

A   B   C   D   E

Reflected shapes

In **reflected** shape questions you need to recognise **symmetry**. Symmetry is where everything about a picture stays the same but it is the opposite way round – a mirror **image**. When looking for a mirror image, remember that nothing about the shape changes. Its colour and size stay the same and it is not **rotated**. All that happens is that it is reflected in a mirror line.

Copy the image below onto a piece of paper. Then paint over the left-hand arrow. While the paint is wet, fold the paper down the mirror line to make a print. Look at the new image. Imagine that you are doing this for each question that involves reflection.

Simple shapes

When you look in a mirror, everything looks the opposite way round. If you wave your right hand, your left hand seems to wave back. When shapes are reflected they can look as if they have been flipped over.

For example:

Here the arrow on the left looks as though it has been flipped over to create the arrow on the right – its reflection – because it is facing in a different direction.

 Draw the mirror image of these shapes.

1.

3.

2.

4.

Hint If you come across a picture that is on the other side of the mirror line, or if the mirror line is **horizontal**, turn the page round. Then the picture will look like those you know best.

Reflected shapes

Distance from the mirror line

This is another way of working out what a reflection will look like. You need to look carefully at how far certain parts of the picture are from the mirror line.

For example: The picture below is made up of several parts, including a semi-circle and a triangle. The notes explain one way of working out the appearance of the reflected shape.

The **semi-circle** is **furthest** from the mirror line and is at the **top** of the picture.

When the picture is reflected, the **semi-circle** remains **furthest** from the mirror line and at the **top** of the picture.

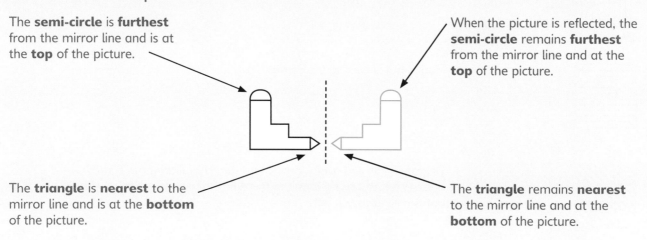

The **triangle** is **nearest** to the mirror line and is at the **bottom** of the picture.

The **triangle** remains **nearest** to the mirror line and at the **bottom** of the picture.

Hint Look carefully at where parts of the shape are in relation to the mirror line. If they are close to it on one side of the line, they will also be close to it on the other.

Use the method described above to find the correct reflection.

1. Notice in the first picture that the black circle is close to the mirror line and the white square is far from the mirror line.

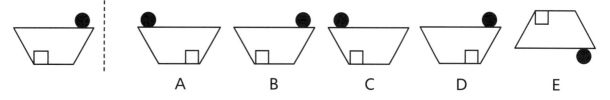

2. Notice in the first picture that the arrow head is close to the mirror line and the crosses are closer to the mirror line than the arrow stem is.

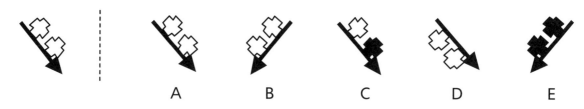

Reflected shapes

When looking at **reflected** shapes you need to check that any patterns are reflected correctly. Lined patterns that are **vertical** or **horizontal** will stay the same. If the pattern is made up of **diagonal** lines, they will appear to flip over and change direction in the reflected shape.

For example:

Vertical lines stay the same.

Horizontal lines stay the same.

Diagonal lines flip over. In the left-hand shape they run from bottom left to top right and in the right-hand shape they run from bottom right to top left.

So as well as imagining the shapes flipping over, you need to imagine the patterns doing the same.

Find the correct reflection. Circle the letter.

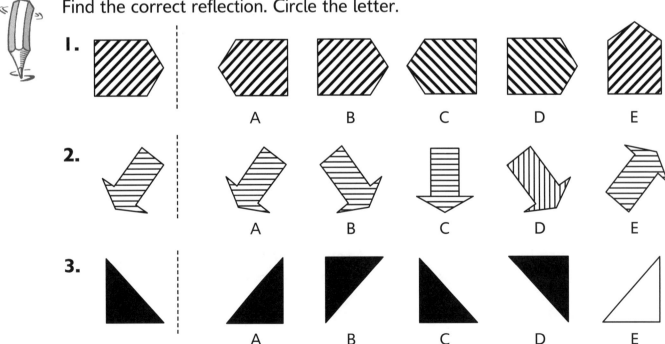

1.   A   B   C   D   E

2.   A   B   C   D   E

3.   A   B   C   D   E

Which picture on the right is a reflection of the picture on the left? Circle the letter. If you get stuck, go back to pages 44 to 46 for some reminders.

1.

  A   B   C   D   E

2.

  A   B   C   D   E

3.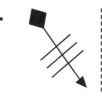

  A   B   C   D   E

4.

  A   B   C   D   E

5.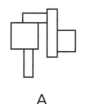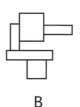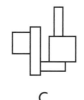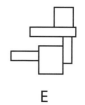

  A   B   C   D   E

6.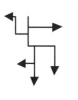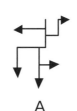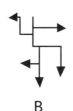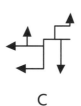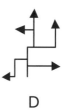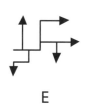

  A   B   C   D   E

Which picture on the right is a **reflection** of the picture on the left?
Circle the letter.

1.

A B C D E

2.

A B C D E

3.

A B C D E

4.

A B C D E

5.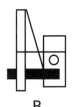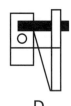

A B C D E

6.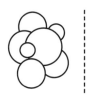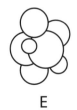

A B C D E

Which picture on the right is a reflection of the picture on the left?
Circle the letter.

1.

     A   B   C   D   E

2.

     A   B   C   D   E

3.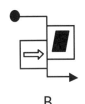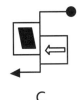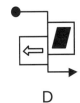

     A   B   C   D   E

4.

     A   B   C   D   E

5.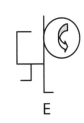

     A   B   C   D   E

6.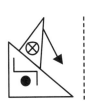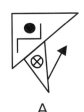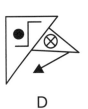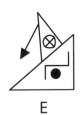

     A   B   C   D   E

Which picture on the right is a **reflection** of the picture on the left?
Circle the letter.

1.

    A   B   C   D   E

2.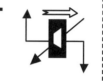

    A   B   C   D   E

3.

    A   B   C   D   E

4.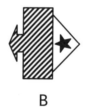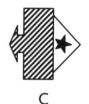

    A   B   C   D   E

5.

    A   B   C   D   E

6.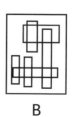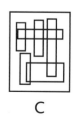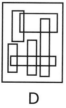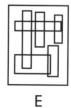

    A   B   C   D   E

Nets of cubes

In nets of cubes questions you need to match the **net** (a flattened 2-D outline of a 3-D shape) of a **cube** to its formed cube. You also have to match a cube to its net. The nets and cubes have patterns on them and these need to be matched up exactly. The most common types of net are shown below.

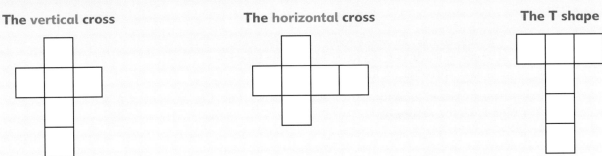

The vertical cross   **The horizontal cross**   **The T shape**

Take a blank piece of thin card or graph paper and copy onto it the nets of cubes shown above. Then cut round each shape. Use the shapes to practise folding nets. You will soon see how the sides of the nets join to make a cube. Try drawing shapes or patterns on each face. While you are learning to do nets questions, use your models to check your answers.

There are three main things to keep in mind when you are answering nets of cubes questions.

Opposites

When nets are folded, **alternate** (next but one) faces will always be opposite each other in the cube. They will never be next to each other.

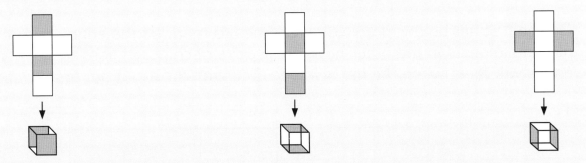

Remembering this will help you to work out:

- where faces on the net should appear on the cube
- where faces on the cube should appear on the net.

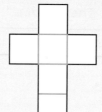

Edges

When the **net** is folded into a **cube** it creates 12 edges. You need to work out which edges on the net go together to make which edges on the cube. Some edges are more obvious as they are already joined on the net.

The blue lines show where faces of the net are already joined. When the net is folded, the blue lines will form the edges of the cube.

You also need to picture which edges will meet as you fold the net.

The blue lines on the following nets show which edges will meet when a cube is formed. Make paper nets based on these diagrams and fold them to see for yourself.

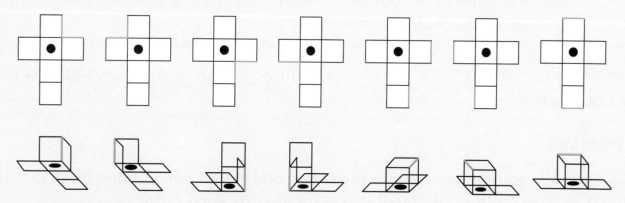

On the first net below, draw coloured lines to mark all the edges that are already joined. On the other nets, draw pairs of coloured lines to show where edges will meet when the net is folded. Try with a cut-out net first if it helps.

I.

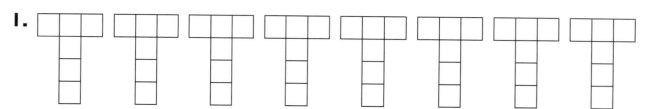

The same rules apply when you open out a cube to make a net. You need to know where the edges that were touching in the cube will be once it is flattened to become a net.

Nets of cubes

Rotated faces

When you fold a net to make a cube, the faces move. Sometimes the picture on a face appears to **rotate**. Look at the example below and note what happens to the blue arrow when the lowest face is folded up.

The blue arrow faces down ...   ... then it faces forwards ...   ... then it faces up.

 Draw some pictures on each face of a paper net. See how the pictures appear to rotate as you fold and unfold it.

 Draw the picture as it will appear when the net is folded into a cube.

1. 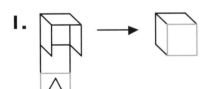   **2.**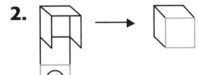

3.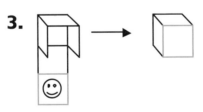

! The same rules apply when you open out a cube to make a net. You need to think about whether the pictures on the cube will have rotated once it is flattened to become a net.

Hint Look at what particular shapes point to. The arrow faces the black square in the net below. It still faces the black square when the net is folded.

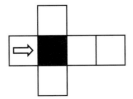

Which **cube** can be made exactly from the **net**? Circle the letter. If you get stuck, go back to pages 51 to 53 for some reminders.

1.

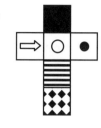

   A   B   C   D   E

2.

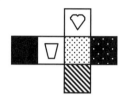

   A   B   C   D   E

3.

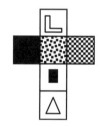

   A   B   C   D   E

Which net can be made exactly from the cube? Circle the letter.

4.

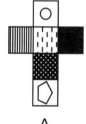   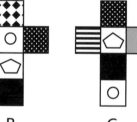   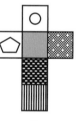   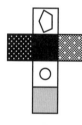

   A   B   C   D   E

5.

   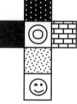   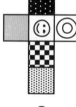      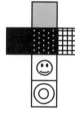

   A   B   C   D   E

6.

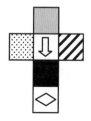   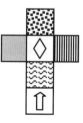   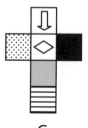   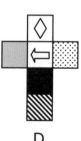   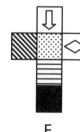

   A   B   C   D   E

Which cube can be made exactly from the net? Circle the letter.

1.

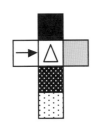

 A B C D   E

2.

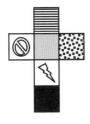

 A B C D E

3.

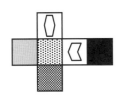

 A B C D E

Which net can be made exactly from the cube? Circle the letter.

4.

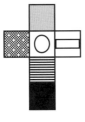

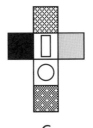 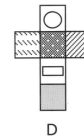 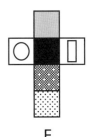

A   B   C   D   E

5.

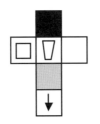 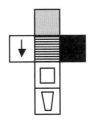 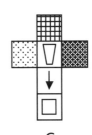 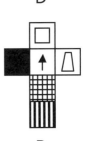 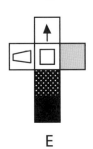

A   B   C   D   E

6.

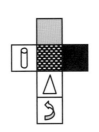 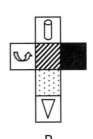 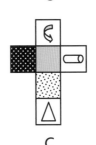 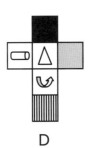 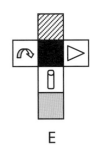

A   B   C   D   E

Which **cube** can be made exactly from the **net**? Circle the letter.

1.

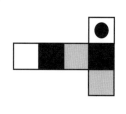

A   B   C   D   E

2.

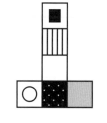

A   B   C   D   E

3.

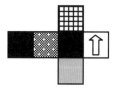

A   B   C   D   E

 Which net can be made exactly from the cube? Circle the letter.

4.

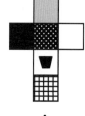 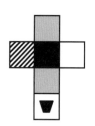 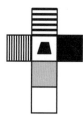 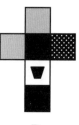 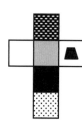

A   B   C   D   E

5.

 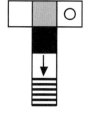 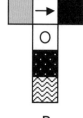 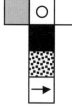 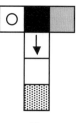 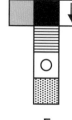

A   B   C   D   E

6.

  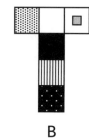 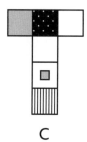 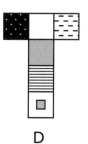 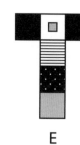

A   B   C   D   E

Which cube can be made exactly from the net? Circle the letter.

1.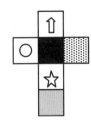

  A   B   C   D   E

2.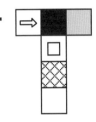

  A   B   C   D   E

3.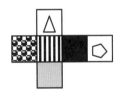

  A   B   C   D   E

 Which net can be made exactly from the cube? Circle the letter.

4.

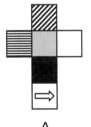 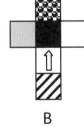 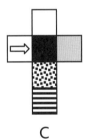 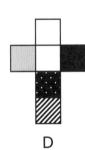 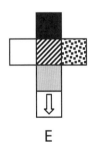

  A   B   C   D   E

5.

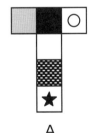 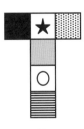 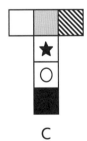 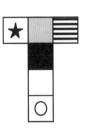 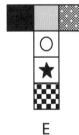

  A   B   C   D   E

6.

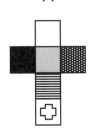 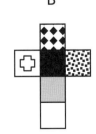 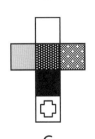 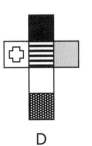 

  A   B   C   D   E

Codes

In non-verbal reasoning, **codes** are letters that are used to describe pictures. Each picture has two letters beneath it. Each letter describes one part of the picture. You are given several pictures, each of which has a two-letter code. You need to work out what each letter is describing. Then you find the code that describes a final additional picture. You are always given a choice of codes from which to pick your answer.

Hint Look for the feature that pictures with the same letter have **in common**.

For example:

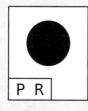   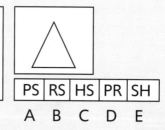

A B C D E

The final picture is a **white triangle**. You have just worked out that **H** is **white** and **S** is **triangle** so the code must be **HS**.

The first two pictures both start with the letter **P. What do they have in common?** They are both shaded **black**. The first letter must describe the **colour**. **P** is **black** so the **H** in the third picture must mean **white**.

The first and third pictures both end with the letter **R. What do they have in common?** They are both **circles**. The second letter must describe the **shape**. **R** is a **circle** so the **S** in the second picture must mean **triangle**.

Answer: C

Work out what feature each letter describes and write the feature below. Circle the code for the final picture.

I.

 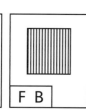 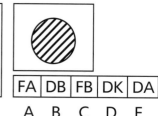

A B C D E

F = _____

D = _____

B = _____

K = _____

Codes

As the questions get harder you are given more pictures, with more features.

For example:

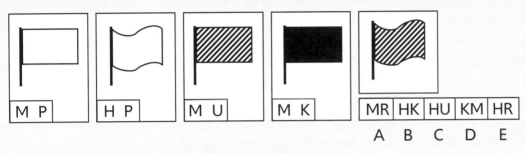

First letter
M = straight rectangle
H = wavy.

Second letter
P = white
U = striped
K = black.

Three pictures have **M** as their first letter. What do they have **in common**? The flags are straight rectangles. The **first** letter must describe the flag **shape**.

The first two pictures have **P** as their second letter. What do they have **in common**? Both flags are **white**. The **second** letter must describe the flag **colour**.

The final picture is a **wavy** flag that is **striped**. **H** is **wavy** and **U** is **stripy** so the code must be **HU**.

Answer: C

Work out what feature each letter describes and write the feature below. Circle the code for the final picture.

I.

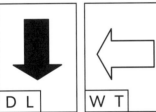 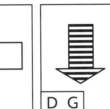  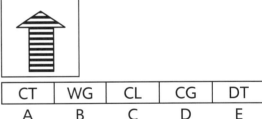

D = _____

W = _____

C = _____

L = _____

T = _____

G = _____

What is the **code** of the final picture? Circle the letter. If you get stuck, go back to pages 58 and 59 for some reminders.

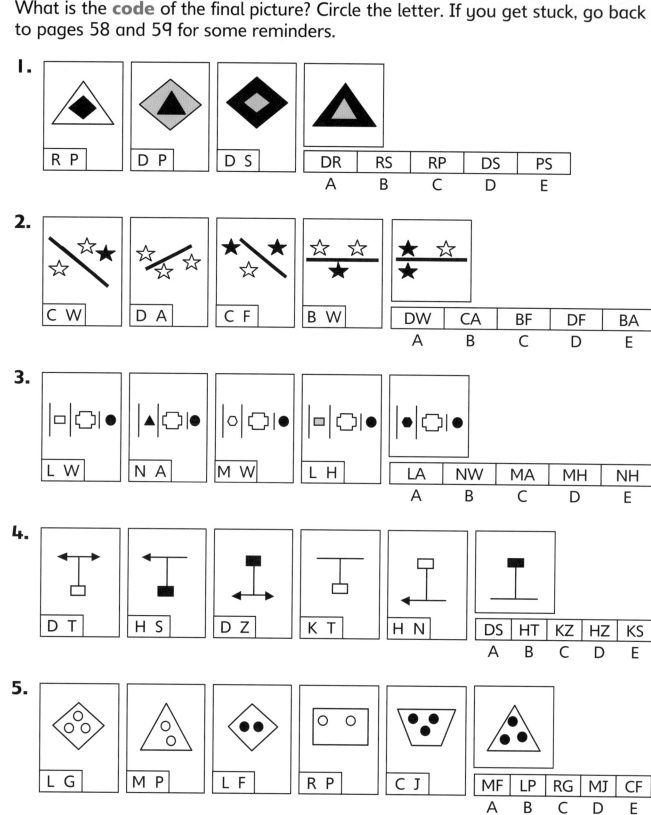

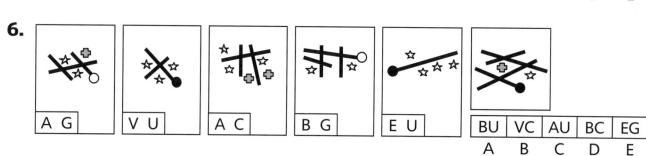

What is the code of the final picture? Circle the letter.

1.

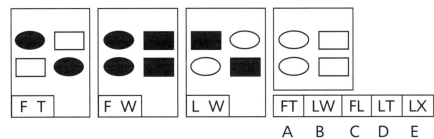

A   B   C   D   E

2.

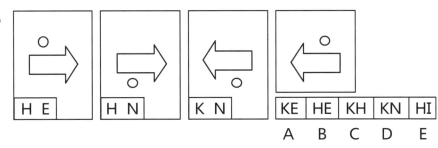

A   B   C   D   E

3.

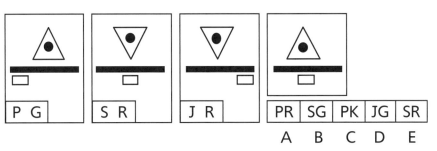

A   B   C   D   E

4.

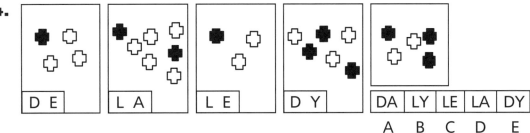

A   B   C   D   E

5.

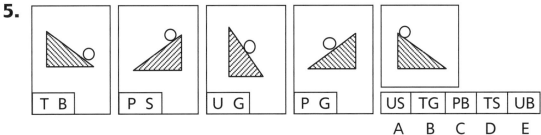

A   B   C   D   E

6.

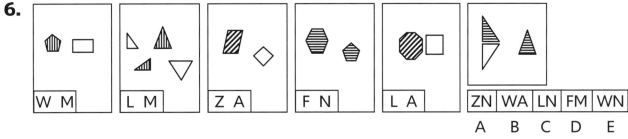

A   B   C   D   E

What is the **code** of the final picture? Circle the letter.

1.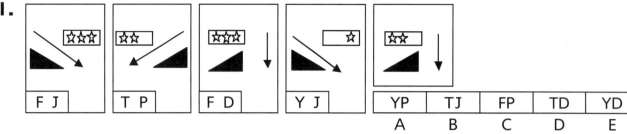

					YP	TJ	FP	TD	YD
F J	T P	F D	Y J		A	B	C	D	E

2.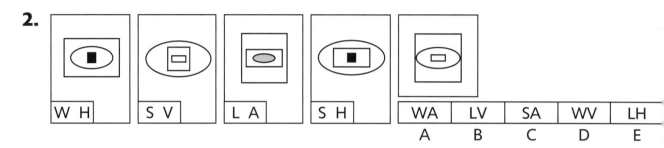

					WA	LV	SA	WV	LH
W H	S V	L A	S H		A	B	C	D	E

3.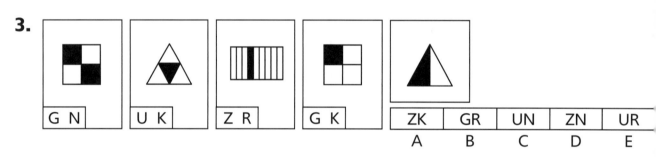

					ZK	GR	UN	ZN	UR
G N	U K	Z R	G K		A	B	C	D	E

4.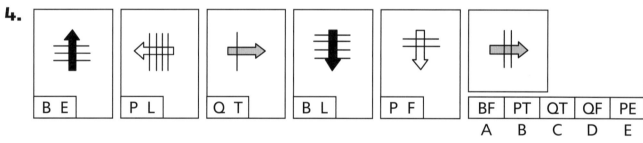

						BF	PT	QT	QF	PE
B E	P L	Q T	B L	P F		A	B	C	D	E

5.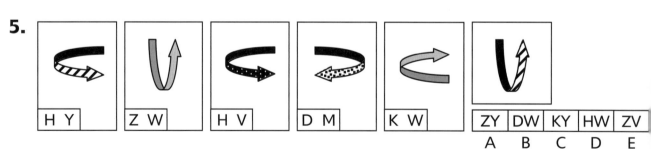

						ZY	DW	KY	HW	ZV
H Y	Z W	H V	D M	K W		A	B	C	D	E

6.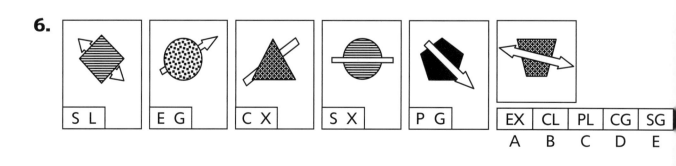

						EX	CL	PL	CG	SG
S L	E G	C X	S X	P G		A	B	C	D	E

What is the code of the final picture? Circle the letter.

1.

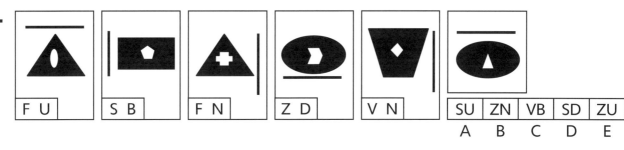

						SU	ZN	VB	SD	ZU
F U	S B	F N	Z D	V N		A	B	C	D	E

2.

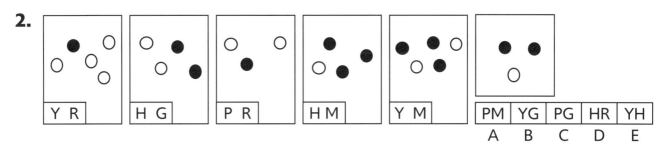

						PM	YG	PG	HR	YH
Y R	H G	P R	H M	Y M		A	B	C	D	E

3.

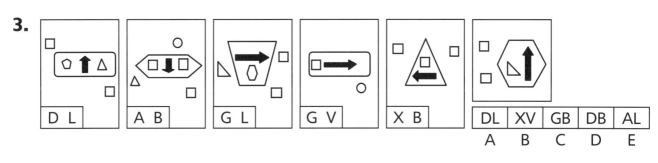

						DL	XV	GB	DB	AL
D L	A B	G L	G V	X B		A	B	C	D	E

4.

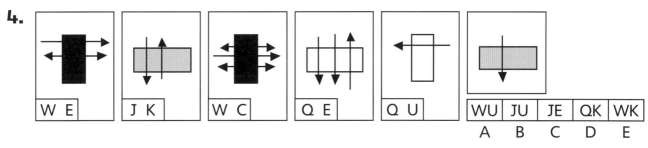

						WU	JU	JE	QK	WK
W E	J K	W C	Q E	Q U		A	B	C	D	E

5.

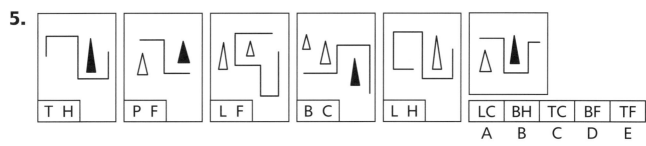

						LC	BH	TC	BF	TF
T H	P F	L F	B C	L H		A	B	C	D	E

6.

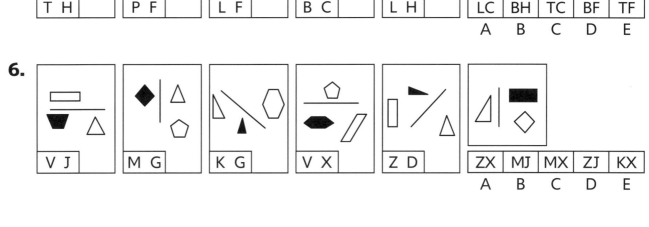

						ZX	MJ	MX	ZJ	KX
V J	M G	K G	V X	Z D		A	B	C	D	E

In **combined** shape questions you are shown two shapes. You have to find the single **image** that is made by putting the two shapes together.

Hint The original shapes never change in size or colour. They are never **reflected**. However, they may **overlap** or be **rotated**.

For example:

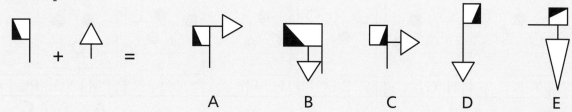

Look very carefully at one shape at a time to see whether it has remained the same.

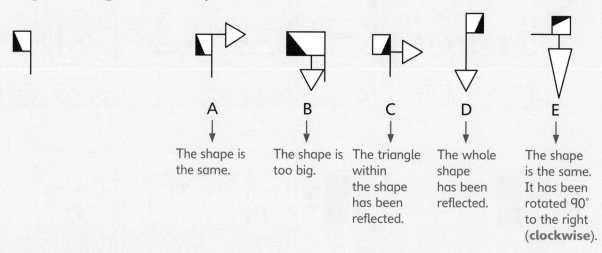

The shape is the same. | The shape is too big. | The triangle within the shape has been reflected. | The whole shape has been reflected. | The shape is the same. It has been rotated 90° to the right (**clockwise**).

Only in **A** and **E** has the first shape remained the same. Now check for the second shape.

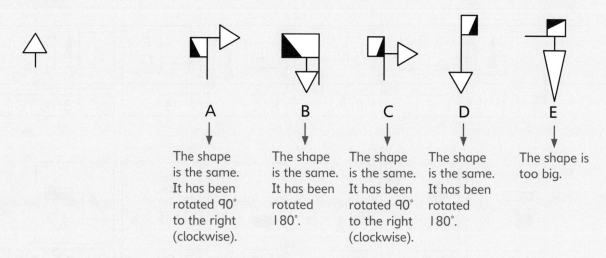

The shape is the same. It has been rotated 90° to the right (clockwise). | The shape is the same. It has been rotated 180°. | The shape is the same. It has been rotated 90° to the right (clockwise). | The shape is the same. It has been rotated 180°. | The shape is too big.

A, **B**, **C** and **D** all contain the second shape. The only image in which both of the shapes stay the same is **A**.

Answer: A

Look carefully at this example.

1.

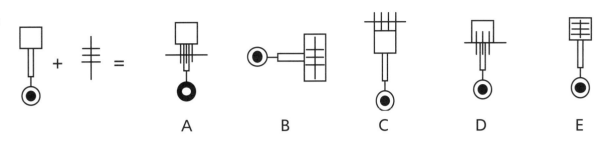

a) Underneath each image, write whether the **first** shape has stayed the same (and possibly rotated) or if it has changed (and if so how).

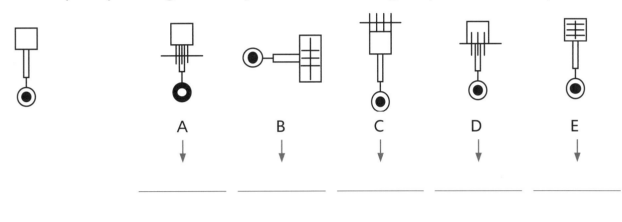

_____ _____ _____ _____ _____

_____ _____ _____ _____ _____

The picture has stayed the same in images _____

b) Now write whether the **second** shape has stayed the same or changed.

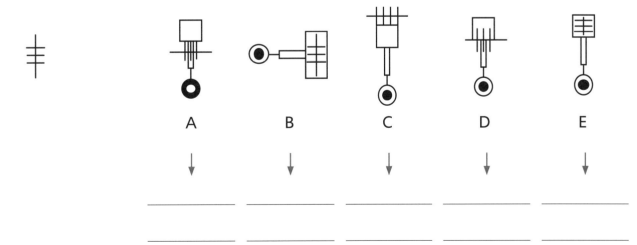

_____ _____ _____ _____ _____

_____ _____ _____ _____ _____

Answer: __

Hint   Once you get used to combined shape questions you will only need to look closely at those images where the first shape stayed the same.

Which picture on the right can be made by combining the first two shapes? Circle the letter. If you get stuck, go back to pages 64 and 65 for some reminders.

1.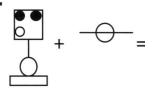

A   B   C   D   E

2.

A   B   C   D   E

3.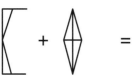

A   B   C   D   E

4.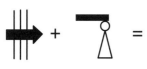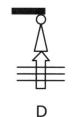

A   B   C   D   E

5.

A   B   C   D   E

6.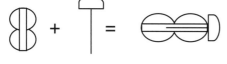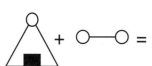

A   B   C   D   E

Which picture on the right can be made by combining the first two shapes? Circle the letter.

1.

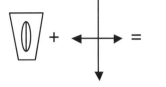  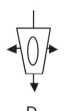 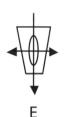

              A   B   C   D   E

2.

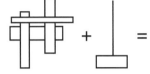   

              A   B   C   D   E

3.

              A   B   C   D   E

4.

              A   B   C   D   E

5.

              A   B   C   D   E

6.

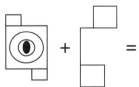 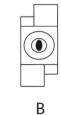

              A   B   C   D   E

Which picture on the right can be made by combining the first two shapes? Circle the letter.

1.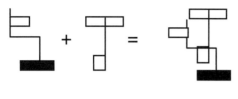

         A   B   C   D   E

2.

         A   B   C   D   E

3.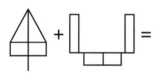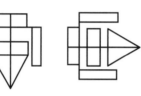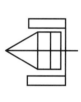

         A   B   C   D   E

4.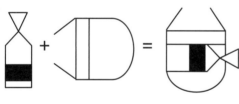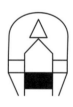

         A   B   C   D   E

5.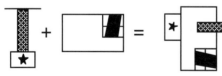

         A   B   C   D   E

6.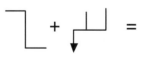

         A   B   C   D   E

Which picture on the right can be made by combining the first two shapes?
Circle the letter.

1.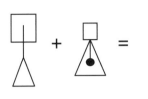

A   B   C   D   E

2.

A   B   C   D   E

3.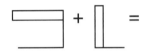

A   B   C   D   E

4.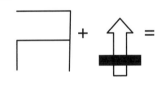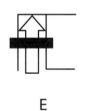

A   B   C   D   E

5.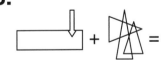

A   B   C   D   E

6.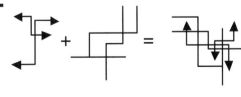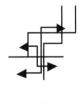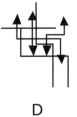

A   B   C   D   E

Page 4 *When answering **similarities** questions you can write the common features in any order you like.*

    1. Common features: White rectangle. (A rectangle is a shape with four straight sides and four **right angles** [angles of 90°].)
                                            White circle inside white rectangle.
                                            Black triangle attached to side of white rectangle.

    2. Common features: Jointed arrow. ('Jointed' means that the line changes direction.)
                                            Small white triangle touching the arrow head.
                                            White triangle touching nothing.
                                            Squiggly black line touching nothing.

Page 5 **1. D** Common features:

White rectangle.	Ⓐ	Ⓑ	Ⓒ	Ⓓ	Ⓔ
White circle in rectangle.	Ⓐ	B	C	Ⓓ	Ⓔ
Black triangle.	A	Ⓑ	Ⓒ	Ⓓ	E

        Only **D** has been circled each time. **D** is the answer.

    2. A Common features:

Jointed arrow.	Ⓐ	B	C	D	Ⓔ
Small white triangle touching arrow.	Ⓐ	B	C	D	Ⓔ
White triangle touching nothing.	Ⓐ	Ⓑ	Ⓒ	Ⓓ	Ⓔ
Squiggly line touching nothing.	Ⓐ	Ⓑ	Ⓒ	D	E

        Only **A** has been circled each time. **A** is the answer.

Page 6 **1. B** **a)** A Ⓑ C D Ⓔ
                b) A Ⓑ Ⓒ Ⓓ E
                c) Ⓐ Ⓑ Ⓒ Ⓓ Ⓔ
                d) Ⓐ Ⓑ Ⓒ D E

        Only **B** has been circled each time. **B** is the answer.

    2. B Common features:

Thin **vertical** line.	**a)**	Ⓐ	Ⓑ	C	Ⓓ	E
White 2-D (two-dimensional) shape containing a white four-headed arrow.	**b)**	Ⓐ	Ⓑ	C	Ⓓ	Ⓔ
Vertical thick black arrows pointing from the top and the bottom of the 2-D shape.	**c)**	A	Ⓑ	Ⓒ	D	Ⓔ

        Only **B** has been circled each time. **B** is the answer.

Page 7   **1. A** – Each picture contains a jointed line with two right angles (angles of 90°), and a hexagon. (A hexagon is a 2-D shape with six sides.)

2. C – Each picture contains a shape where exactly half has been shaded black and the other half is white, and there is a small black circle sitting on the top.

3. A – Each flag contains four stripes of which two are white, as well as a black flagpole.

4. E – Each picture contains a 2-D shape attached to an identical shape which is the same colour but smaller.

5. D – Each picture contains at least one straight line and a curved line that joins but does not cross it.

6. E – Each picture contains a large, irregular shape containing smaller 2-D shapes. The number of sides of the smaller shapes always totals 10.

Page 8   **1. C** – Each picture contains two lines that cross. One of the lines has one black circle on it and the other has two black circles on it. A black arrow crosses one of the lines.

2. D – Each picture contains a large quadrilateral (four-sided shape). The quadrilateral contains three triangles. Two are white, facing in opposite directions, and one is black.

3. B – Each picture shows a large 2-D shape containing a **horizontal** and a vertical line. The lines cross, creating four sections. In one section there is an arrow. The arrow points to another 2-D shape in the opposite section.

4. D – Each picture contains a jointed line with a triangle and a quadrilateral, and one other 2-D shape.

5. D – Each picture contains an even number of circles, half of which are white and half of which are black.

6. B – Each picture contains a **symmetrical image**.

Page 9   **1. C** – Each picture contains a jointed arrow with a curved line crossing it.

2. D – Each picture contains a black oval.

3. D – Each picture contains an arrow that is crossed by a line or lines that are each made of the same thickness and type as the arrow.

4. A – Each picture has an arrow attached to a shape and pointing away from it. The arrow and the shape are the same colour.

5. D – Each picture shows a triangle with a curved section cut out.

6. C – Each picture has lines and/or arrows crossing at five points.

Page 10   **1. B** – Each picture contains two rectangles and two lollipops, one black and one white.

2. B – Each picture contains the same shape in different sizes. All the shapes **overlap**.

3. A – Each picture contains a black star, two different shapes and a jointed line or arrow.

4. C – Each picture contains a large shape and a number of smaller, matching shapes. Count the number of sides that the large shape has. The number of smaller shapes is the same as this number.

5. D – Each picture contains an arrow pointing to a smaller, black version of the bigger shape.

6. D – Each picture contains a black shape sitting on an arrow, with a shorter line on the opposite side of the arrow to the shape, running parallel to the arrow. (Parallel lines are lines that are the same distance apart for their whole length.)

Page 11 **1. B** – The other four are black. **B** is the **odd one out** because it is the only white one.

2. E – The other four arrows are all pointing to the right. **E** is the odd one out because it is the only one pointing to the left.

Page 12 **1.** **A**, **C**, **D** and **E** all have a chequered pattern. (A 'chequered' pattern has light and dark squares, like a chess board.)

2. **A**, **B**, **D** and **E** are all made up of two lines.

3. **A**, **B**, **C** and **E** all have a thick black outline. **D** is the odd one out as it is the only one with a thin black outline.

4. **A**, **B**, **C** and **D** all have arrows pointing into the shape. **E** is the odd one out as it is the only one where the arrow is pointing out of the shape.

5. **A**, **B**, **C** and **E** are all quadrilaterals (four-sided shapes). **D** is the odd one out as it is the only three-sided shape.

Page 13 **1. C** – The other four shapes all have straight sides. **C** is the odd one out as it is the only one with curved sides.

2. D – The other four all have a curly line crossing the straight line. **D** is the odd one out as it has a zigzag line crossing the straight line.

3. D – The other four all have a smaller shape inside the bigger shape. **D** is the odd one out as it does not have a smaller shape inside.

4. B – The other four all have lines that stop on the edge of the shape. **B** is the odd one out as it is the only one where the line passes through both sides of the shape.

5. E – The other four are all six-sided shapes. **E** is the odd one out as it has only five sides.

6. A – The other four all have one white shape, two black shapes and three grey shapes. **A** is the odd one out as it is the only one to have one black shape, two white shapes and three grey shapes.

Page 14 **1. C** – The other four have lines that cross at two places. **C** is the odd one out as the lines only cross once.

2. C – The other four all have a white star in the centre. **C** is the odd one out as it has a black star in the centre.

3. D – The other four all have an arrow pointing up. **D** is the odd one out as it does not have an arrow pointing up.

4. B – The other four all have a total of eight sides. **B** is the odd one out as it only has seven sides.

5. D – The other four have two small shapes the same colour. **D** is the odd one out as it is the only one that does not have two small shapes the same colour.

6. A – The other four all have a circle and an arrow head at either end of the line. **A** is the odd one as it is the only one to have circles at both ends of the line.

Answers

Page 15
1. **E** – The other four arrows are all pointing **anticlockwise**. **E** is the odd one out as it is the only one pointing **clockwise**.

2. **A** – The other four pictures have shapes that are **reflected** along a vertical mirror line. **A** is the odd one out as the arrows are not reflected along a vertical mirror line.

3. **D** – The other four all contain quadrilaterals. **D** is the odd one out as it is the only one that does not contain a quadrilateral.

4. **B** – The other four all have a square, then a circle, then a square, then a triangle going in a clockwise direction around the ring. **B** is the odd one out as it is the only one not to follow this pattern.

5. **C** – The other four are not symmetrical. **C** is the odd one out as it is symmetrical.

6. **D** – The other four all have three black spots and four white spots. **D** is the odd one out as it is the only one with four black spots and three white spots.

Page 16
1. **E** – The other four have all the arrows within the squares facing in the same direction. **E** is the odd one out as it is the only one where one of the arrows points in a different direction to the others in the square.

2. **A** – The other four all have the smaller shape overlapping the edge of the bigger shape. **A** is the odd one out as the smaller shape is completely within the bigger shape.

3. **C** – The other four all have two arrow lines in front of the triangle and one arrow line behind. **C** is the odd one out as it is the only one to have three arrow lines in front of the triangle.

4. **D** – The other four all have shapes with a thick black edge within the oval. **D** is the odd one out as the hexagon (the shape with six sides) does not have a thick black edge.

5. **D** – The other four all have three shapes outside the cross. **D** is the odd one out as it is the only one to have four shapes outside the cross.

6. **B** – The other four all have lines that cross in three places. **B** is the odd one out as it is the only one that has lines that cross in four places.

Page 17
1. Similarity: Both are black right-angled triangles.
Difference: Second triangle is much smaller.

2. Similarity: Same jointed lines.
Difference: Second picture has two lines in the middle rather than just one.

Page 18
1. **C** – Remains a white trapezium but is much smaller. (A trapezium is a four-sided figure with only two parallel sides, and these are of different lengths.)

2. **A** – Has the same jointed line but has two arrows going through the middle rather than just one.

3. **Rotated** 180°.

4. Rotated 90° to the left (anticlockwise) or 270° to the right (clockwise).

Page 19
1. **E** – In the first pair of pictures the arrow changed by rotating 180° and the stripes rotated 90° so the same had to be done with the heart.

2. **B** – The pictures have been reflected in a vertical mirror line.

Answers

Page 20   **1. D** – A large white rectangle becomes a large black rectangle so a large white pentagon must become a large black pentagon. (A pentagon is a 2-D shape with five sides.) No rotations have taken place.

         2. B – A large black heart becomes a large white heart so a large black club must become a large white club. No rotations have taken place.

         3. B – The second picture is the same as the first picture but smaller. **B** is the same as the third picture but smaller.

         4. C – A white left hand becomes a black right hand, so a white left foot becomes a black right foot.

         5. C – A black arrow pointing right has rotated 90° clockwise to become a white arrow pointing down, so a black curved arrow pointing right must rotate 90° clockwise to become a white curved arrow pointing down.

         6. E – A white eight-sided octagon halves its number of sides and changes colour to become a black four-sided square, so a white six-sided hexagon must halve its sides and become a black three-sided triangle.

Page 21   **1. C** – The image is reflected and loses one of the vertical lines.

         2. C – The image is reflected.

         3. E – The image rotates 90° clockwise.

         4. B – The larger shape becomes squashed and turns black. The centre shape remains the same.

         5. D – The top left-hand shape swaps colour with the large shape below, and becomes reflected within the large shape. The top right-hand shape disappears.

         6. B – The image rotates 90° clockwise, the black and white halves swap over and the black circle moves to above the main image.

Page 22   **1. B** – The image has been reflected in a vertical mirror line.

         2. A – The image has been rotated 90° anticlockwise.

         3. D – The thick lines have become thin and the thin lines have become thick.

         4. D – The large shape has been reflected in a horizontal mirror line along with the small left-hand shape, which has changed from white to black. The small right-hand shape has remained in the same position but has been reflected in a horizontal mirror line and changed from black to white.

         5. A – The shapes fit together to create a rectangle and have the same direction of stripes.

         6. B – The image has been rotated 180°.

Page 23   **1. D** – The image has been rotated 180°.

         2. D – The image has been reflected in a vertical mirror line, an extra line has been added to the arrow and the central shape has become white.

         3. A – The jointed line/arrow has been reflected in a vertical mirror line, the four lines/arrows have been reflected in a horizontal mirror line and the black and white shapes have stayed the same, between the wider spaced lines/arrows.

         4. A – The layout of the picture stays the same, but white shapes have become grey, grey shapes have become black and black shapes have become white.

         5. C – The arrow reflects in a horizontal mirror line and moves to the top of the shape, as well as becoming black, and the white shape inside remains the same.

6. A – The shape becomes smaller and the triangle reflects in a horizontal mirror line.

Page 24 1. Lion, dog, lion, dog. *Your drawing should show that the next one in the sequence is a lion.*

2. White arrow facing up, black arrow facing down, white arrow facing up, black arrow facing down. *Your drawing should show that the next one in the sequence is a white arrow pointing up.*

Page 25 1. B – Arrow pointing right with two vertical lines crossing it, white rectangle with black oval inside, arrow pointing right with two vertical lines crossing it, white rectangle with black oval inside. Next one in sequence – arrow pointing right with two vertical lines crossing it.

2. A – Striped triangle inside larger white triangle, chequered rectangle inside larger white rhombus, striped triangle inside larger white triangle, chequered rectangle inside larger white rhombus. (A rhombus is a diamond shape with four equal sides and no right angles.) Next one in sequence – striped triangle inside larger white triangle.

Page 26 1. Similarities: White rectangle.
Triangle on top of the rectangle.
Differences: Number of **diagonal** stripes within the rectangle increasing by one each time.
Triangle changing from black to white to black and so on – a repeating pattern.
Answer: **B** White rectangle with a white triangle on top and four diagonal lines inside.

2. Similarities: Thick-rimmed circle.
Thin arrow inside circle.
Differences: Colour of circle changing from black to grey in a repeating pattern.
Arrow rotating 90° clockwise each time.
Perpendicular lines on arrow reducing by one each time.
Answer: **E** Arrow pointing right with three perpendicular lines inside a grey circle.

Page 27 1. B – Repeating pattern of white sun on spotted background and white star with black spot inside.

2. D – Triangles are gradually getting smaller and the slight increase in the number of dots within makes them appear to be getting slightly darker each time as well.

3. A – Circles show a repeating pattern of white, black, white and the white triangles around the edge are increasing by one each time.

4. A – A horizontal line from the top left is moving to the bottom right from one picture to the next.

5. E – The rectangle is getting gradually bigger in each picture and the number of black circles on top is increasing by one each time.

6. B – The circle within the black rectangle is gradually moving along the length of the rectangle and is also getting darker from one picture to the next. The arch is gradually moving around the edge of the rectangle.

Answers

Page 28 **1. E** – The white leaf is moving clockwise around the clover, one leaf at a time.
2. C – The number of lines is increasing by one each time.
3. E – The arrow is rotating 45° clockwise and alternating between white and black.
4. D – The image is rotating 90° clockwise.
5. C – The image is rotating 45° clockwise.
6. A – An extra triangle is added each time.

Page 29 **1. C** – The number of shapes on the oval is increasing by one each time and alternating between black triangles and white diamonds.
2. E – The image is rotating approximately 20° clockwise in each picture.
3. B – The number of sides each shape has increases by one in each picture and the number of lines around the shape equals the number of sides it has.
4. C – This is a repeating pattern.
5. A – The size of the square is getting smaller in each picture, as are the number of circles. There is one black circle in each picture.
6. D – The position of the triangle shows a repeating pattern and in each picture one star moves from inside the triangle to outside it.

Page 30 **1. A** – This is a repeating pattern of a triangle with a four-sided shape within it and a circle with a total of eight sides within it.
2. B – The jointed line is rotating 90° clockwise each time and the number of arrows is increasing by one (it is not **D** because the arrows are at the wrong end of the jointed line).
3. E – The lines within the square are rotating 45° clockwise, alternating between fuzzy and solid, and the circle is gradually getting smaller.
4. A – The circle is rotating 45° anticlockwise and a black circle is added each time to the right of the previous black circle.
5. B – The number of sides is increasing by three each time and there is at least one black shape.
6. D – The curved arrow is rotating 90° clockwise and the straight arrow is rotating 90° anticlockwise.

Page 31 **1. C** – Shape is in the same position.

Page 32 **1. C** – Shape is rotated 45° clockwise.
2. A – Shape is rotated 45° clockwise.
3. D – Shape is rotated 135° clockwise.
4. C – Shape is rotated 45° clockwise.

Page 33 **1. A** – Shape is in the same position.
2. B – Shape is in the same position.
3. E – Shape is rotated 90°.
4. D – Shape is rotated 135° clockwise.
5. B – Shape is in the same position.
6. A – Shape is rotated 90° clockwise.

Page 34 **1. A** – Shape is in the same position.
2. C – Shape is in the same position.

3. **C** – Shape is rotated 90° anticlockwise.
4. **A** – Shape is in the same position.
5. **B** – Shape is in the same position.
6. **D** – Shape is rotated 90° clockwise.

Page 35 1. **A** – Shape is in the same position.
2. **E** – Shape is rotated 90° clockwise.
3. **B** – Shape is in the same position.
4. **A** – Shape is rotated 180°.
5. **C** – Shape is rotated 180°.
6. **A** – Shape is rotated 180°.

Page 36 1. **A** – Shape is rotated 180°.
2. **B** – Shape is rotated 90° clockwise.
3. **C** – Shape is rotated 90° anticlockwise.
4. **A** – Shape is rotated 90° (clockwise or anticlockwise).
5. **B** – Shape is rotated 90° clockwise.
6. **C** – Shape is rotated 90° (clockwise or anticlockwise).

Page 37 1. **Row** 1 – Black 2-D shapes.
Row 2 – Grey 2-D shapes.
Row 3 – White 2-D shapes.
Column 1 – Rectangles getting smaller and changing from black to grey to white.
Column 2 – Triangles getting smaller and changing from black to grey to white.
Column 3 – Circles getting smaller and changing from black to grey to white.
Answer: **D**

Page 38 1. **A** – All the tails face the centre of the picture.
2. **B** – The black rectangles are always on the outer edge of the picture. The white rectangles are always towards the centre of the picture.

Page 39 1. **A** – Rotating 90° clockwise (the arrow heads are all pointing to the centre).
2. **C** – Rotating 90° clockwise (the feet always point to the centre).

Page 40 1. **B** – The repeating pattern of the rows – heart, club, spade – gradually get smaller in each column.
2. **B** – The repeating pattern of the rows – white outer shape with black inner shape, black outer shape with white inner shape, white outer shape with black inner shape – with the shapes changing through the columns – circle and square, to square and circle, to triangle and diamond.
3. **A** – The top two mice are reflected in a horizontal mirror line to create the bottom two mice (noses all pointing to the sides).
4. **D** – The top two leaves are reflected in a horizontal mirror line to create the bottom two leaves (tips of leaves all pointing to the centre).
5. **B** – The monkeys are rotated 90° clockwise, from top left to top right to bottom right to bottom left (the tails are always in the centre).
6. **E** – The ladybirds are rotated 90° anticlockwise from top left to top right to bottom right to bottom left (the legs are all on the left-hand side of the head).

Answers

Page 41 **1. B** – The top two circles are reflected in a horizontal mirror line to create the bottom circles. Also, the left-hand circles are reflected in a vertical mirror line to create the right-hand circles.

2. E – The dog is rotating 90° clockwise moving from top left to top right to bottom right to bottom left (back paws always in the centre).

3. D – The left-hand shape of the row gets bigger, is reflected in a horizontal mirror line and turns black to become the right-hand shape.

4. E – In each row the shapes **alternate** between black and white and are reflected in a horizontal mirror line each time.

5. C – In each row the images are rotating approximately 20° clockwise each time.

6. B – The entire picture is symmetrical along a central horizontal or vertical line.

Page 42 **1. B** – The top row is reflected in a horizontal mirror line to make the bottom row and there is a change of colour from white to black.

2. D – The image is rotating 90° clockwise moving from top left to top right to bottom right to bottom left (the arrow is always pointing to the L-shaped image in the centre).

3. E – The image is rotating 90° anticlockwise moving from top left to top right to bottom right to bottom left. You could also look at it as though the entire picture had been reflected in a diagonal mirror line.

4. B – The images in the first and last box in each row are mirror images of each other.

5. B – The four rectangular corner images are rotating 90° clockwise moving from top left to top right to bottom right to bottom left. The thin arrow is always pointing into the centre and goes behind the rectangle.

6. D – The rows contain circles, triangles then squares. As the images go down the columns, the shapes get smaller and the number of squares around them increases by one each time.

Page 43 **1. B** – In each row the image has rotated 90° clockwise and got bigger.

2. C – The entire picture can be seen as symmetrical along a central horizontal or vertical line.

3. B – The entire picture can be seen as symmetrical along a central horizontal or vertical line.

4. A – In each column the number of shapes within the large shape is increasing by one each time and the larger shape is getting darker in colour.

5. C – In each row, the shape is rotating 90° clockwise and the small arrow is rotating 90° anticlockwise.

6. C – The squares with the arrows in are rotating 90° clockwise.

Page 44 **1.** 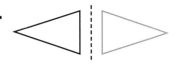   **3.**

2. 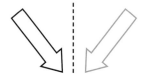   **4.**

Page 45 **1. A** – The black circle is still near the mirror line and on top of the trapezium. The white square is still far away from the mirror line and within the bottom of the trapezium.

2. B – The arrow is still pointing down and towards the line. The crosses are still on the top of the arrow line.

Page 46 **1. C** – The point of the arrow is still facing the mirror line. The diagonal stripes have reflected and so now run top left to bottom right rather than top right to bottom left.

2. B – The arrow is still facing away from the mirror line towards the bottom. The horizontal lines have remained horizontal.

3. A – The right-angled corner of the triangle is still far away from the mirror line and is at the bottom of the picture.

Page 47 **1. B** – The right-angled corner is still far from the mirror line at the bottom. The ball is at the top of the triangle and far from the mirror line. The diagonal lines have reflected and so now run top right to bottom left rather than top left to bottom right.

2. B – The wider end of the 'L' shape is still close to the mirror line and has the small black square attached to the bottom, very close to the mirror line. The small black right-angled triangle is still far from the mirror line at the bottom. The diagonal lines of the right-angled triangle have reflected so now run top left to bottom right rather than top right to bottom left.

3. A – The arrow head is still close to the mirror line, pointing towards the bottom.

4. B – The point of the equilateral triangle is still pointing towards the mirror line at the bottom of the picture. The black arch is still at the top, close to the mirror line. The arch is attached to the white rectangle, which in turn is attached to the thick black line. This thick black line is still furthest away from the mirror line. The horizontal stripes remain horizontal.

5. D – If you follow the shapes around, you still have the long thin rectangle closest to the mirror line at the bottom, attached to the large square, which is attached to the vertical rectangle. This is then attached to the long horizontal rectangle, which has the smaller square on top near the mirror line. It is not **E** because the top square is at the wrong end of the line.

6. A – The arrows facing towards the mirror line are still facing the mirror line. Those facing away from the mirror line are still facing away.

Page 48 **1. C** – Not only has the shape reflected, but the diagonal lines have been reflected as well.

2. D – The circle and triangle are still closest to the mirror line and the vertical rectangle is still furthest away.

3. A – The horizontal arrow is still pointing towards the mirror line. The thick vertical arrow pointing upwards is still closer to the mirror line than the thin vertical arrow pointing downwards.

4. C – The square is still above the diagonal line. The diagonal line is still closest to the mirror line at the bottom and the circles are still in the same colour order, with the two black circles at each end.

5. C – The rectangular shape containing the white circle is still furthest away from the mirror line. The horizontal black rectangle is still behind the thin, vertical, white rectangle.

6. B – The circles that were in front of others in the original image are still in front and those that were behind are still behind.

Page 49 1. B – The top white arrow is furthest away from the mirror line but pointing at it and the bottom arrow is closest to the mirror line and pointing away from it.

2. D – Both triangles have their vertical edge closest to the central line of the image, with the white triangle closest to the mirror line and the black triangle furthest away from the mirror line.

3. A – The black circle is furthest away from the mirror line at the top, the top of the parallelogram is leaning towards the mirror line, the white arrow is pointing away from the mirror line and the thin black arrow is at the bottom pointing to the mirror line. (A parallelogram is a four-sided figure with its opposite side parallel to each other and equal in length.)

4. E – The central arrow is pointing diagonally up and towards the mirror line. The two other arrows are pointing diagonally down and towards the circle.

5. A – The circle is closest to the mirror line with the arrow inside pointing away from the mirror line. The jointed lines are still pointing to the mirror line if that was their original direction, or away from the mirror line if that was their original direction.

6. E – The arrow is still pointing diagonally down towards the mirror line. The large right-angled triangle still has the right angle at the bottom, furthest away from the mirror line, and the black circle is still beneath the jointed line.

Page 50 1. B – The arrow is still pointing towards the mirror line. The stripes have reflected so that within the rectangle they are still sloping down and away from the mirror line. Within the oval the stripes are still sloping down and towards the mirror line.

2. D – The white arrow is still pointing towards the mirror line and the wide edge of the trapezium is still facing the mirror line. The downward-facing arrow of the jointed arrow is still closest to the mirror line. The upwards-facing arrow is still furthest away and the diagonal arrow is still pointing down and away from the mirror line.

3. A – The curved arrow is still pointing down and away from the mirror line and the black arrow is still pointing towards the mirror line. The right angle of the triangle is still at the bottom of the triangle and furthest away from the mirror line.

4. B – The arrow is still pointing at the mirror line and only one point of the star is facing the mirror line. The stripes are still sloping down towards the mirror line.

5. A – All the arrows are still facing the mirror line, with the smaller jointed arrow still at the bottom. The black circle is still closest to the mirror line and attached to the jointed line that still forms the base of the shape.

6. D – The deepest horizontal rectangle is still at the top and has a vertical rectangle overlapping it at the end nearest the mirror line. The three other vertical rectangles are still at the bottom, with the smallest nearest the mirror line and the biggest furthest away.

Page 52 1. *The first **net** below shows the edges that are already joined, **before** you fold the net. Each of the other marked nets in this question should show the pairs of lines that meet when you fold it. You can mark the nets in any order.*

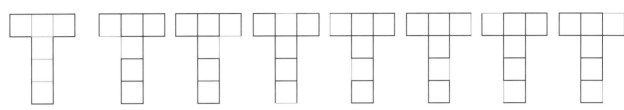

Page 53 1.

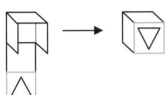

2.

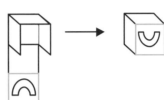

3.

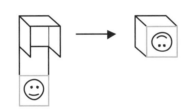

Page 54 1. A – The arrow is pointing towards the circle.
    2. B – The base of the heart is pointing towards the black dots.
    3. C – The base of the triangle is next to the 'L' shape.
    4. A – The side of the hexagon is facing the spots.
    5. C – The top of the face is nearest the circles.
    6. D – The sharpest corner of the diamond is facing the side of the arrow.

Page 55 1. A – The arrow is pointing towards the triangle.
    2. C – The grey square has the zigzag line along one side and the circle along the next side.
    3. C – The arrow shape is pointing away from the black square.
    4. B – The circle is next to the long side of the rectangle, not the short side.
    5. E – The arrow head is pointing away from the white square. The wide end of the trapezium is closest to the square.
    6. D – The arrow is curving up towards the base of the triangle. The circular face of the cylinder is pointing towards the side of the triangle. (A cylinder is a 3-D tube, with parallel sides and circular ends.)

Page 56 1. C – The two grey sides are next to one another.
    2. B – The vertical lines are next to the black square.
    3. C – The arrow points along the side of the black square rather than at or away from it.
    4. C – The wide edge of the trapezium is nearest the grey square.
    5. D – The arrow is pointing away from the black square.

6. A – The stripes are perpendicular to the black square with the white dots.

Page 57 1. B – The arrow is pointing towards the grey square.
    2. A – The arrow is pointing towards the black square.
    3. B – The base of the pentagon is facing the black square.
    4. C – The arrow is pointing towards the black square.
    5. E – The single point of the star is pointing towards the circle.
    6. C – The square with the cross is next to the black square.

Page 58 1. D

Both pictures starting **F** are squares, so the first letter must describe the shape:
F = square   **D** = circle.

Both pictures ending **B** have vertical stripes, so the second letter must describe the direction of the stripe:
B = vertical stripes   **K** = diagonal stripes.

DK = circle with diagonal stripes.

Page 59 1. D

Both pictures starting **D** have an arrow facing down, so the first letter must describe the direction of the arrow:
D = arrow facing down   **W** = arrow facing left
C = arrow facing up.

Both pictures ending **L** are black, so the second letter must describe the colour:
L = black   **T** = white
G = horizontal stripes.

CG = arrow facing up with horizontal stripes.

Page 60 1. B

Both pictures starting **D** have large outer diamonds so the first letter must describe the outer shape:
D = diamond   **R** = triangle.

Both pictures ending **P** have black inner shapes, so the second letter must describe the colour of the inner shape:
P = black   **S** = grey.

RS = triangular outer shape with grey inner shape.

2. C

Both pictures starting **C** have a diagonal line going from top left to bottom right, so the first letter must describe the direction of the line:
C = diagonal from top left to   **D** = diagonal from bottom left to top
    bottom right   right
B = horizontal.

Both pictures ending **W** have one black star and two white stars, so the second letter must describe the number of black and white stars:
W = one black and two white stars   **A** = three white stars
F = two black stars and one white star.

BF = horizontal line with two black stars and one white star.

3. C

Both pictures starting **L** have a rectangle as the shape after the first vertical line, so the first letter must describe the first shape:

L = rectangle **N** = triangle

M = hexagon.

In both pictures ending **W** the first shape is white so the second letter must describe the colour of the first shape:

W = white **A** = black

H = grey.

MA = black hexagon as the first shape after the first vertical line.

4. C

Both pictures starting **D** have double-headed arrows attached to the rectangle, so the first letter must describe the type of line attached to the rectangle:

D = double-headed arrow **H** = single-headed arrow

K = plain line (no arrow heads).

Both pictures ending **T** have a white rectangle under the line, so the second letter must describe the colour and position of the rectangle:

T = white rectangle under the line **S** = black rectangle under the line

Z = black rectangle above the line **N** = white rectangle above the line.

KZ = plain line with a black rectangle above the line.

5. D

Both pictures starting **L** are diamonds, so the first letter must describe the outer shape:

L = diamond **M** = triangle

R = rectangle **C** = trapezium.

(A diamond shape may also be called a rhombus. It has four equal sides and no right angles.)

Both pictures ending **P** have two white circles inside the outer shape, so the second letter must describe the number and colour of circles inside the outer shape:

P = two white circles **G** = three white circles

F = two black circles **J** = three black circles.

MJ = triangle with three black circles in.

6. A

Both pictures starting **A** have three black lines so the first letter must describe the number of black lines:

A = three lines **V** = two lines

B = four lines **E** = one line.

Both pictures ending **G** have a white circle at the end of one of the lines, so the second letter must describe the colour of the circle:

G = white circle **U** = black circle

C = no circle.

BU = four lines with a black circle on the end of one of them.

Page 61 1. D

Both pictures starting **F** have black ovals so the first letter must be the colour of the oval:

F = black oval   **L** = white oval.

Both pictures ending **W** have black rectangles so the second letter must be the colour of the rectangle:

W = black rectangle   **T** = white rectangle.

LT = white ovals and white rectangles.

2. A

Both pictures starting **H** have the arrow head pointing to the right so the first letter must be the direction of the arrow:

H = arrow pointing right   **K** = arrow pointing left.

Both pictures ending with **N** have the circle underneath the arrow. Therefore the second letter must be the position of the circle:

N = circle underneath   **E** = circle above.

KE = arrow pointing left with circle above.

3. B

Both pictures ending **R** have the point of the triangle facing the line so the second letter must be the direction the triangle is pointing:

R = triangle pointing down   **G** = triangle pointing up.

None of the first letters are the same. The only part of the pictures that is not the same is the position of the rectangle under the line:

P = rectangle at the left end of   **S** = rectangle in the centre of the line
the line

J = rectangle at the right end of the line.

SG = rectangle in the centre of the line with the triangle pointing up.

4. B

Both pictures starting **D** have an even number of crosses and both starting **L** have an odd number so the first letter must be the number of crosses:

D = even number of crosses   **L** = odd number of crosses.

Both pictures ending **E** have one black cross so the last letter must be the number of black crosses:

E = one black cross   **A** = two black crosses
Y = three black crosses.

LY = odd number of crosses with three black ones.

5. D

Both pictures starting **P** have the right-angled part of the triangle to the right of the box with the longer edge along the bottom so the first letter must be the position of the triangle:

P = right-angled corner to the right, long edge at the bottom

T = right-angled corner to the left, long edge at the bottom

U = right-angled corner to the left, long edge to the left.

Both pictures ending **G** have the white circle midway down the diagonal edge of the triangle so the second letter must be the position of the circle:

G = circle midway along diagonal edge of triangle

B = circle at the bottom of diagonal edge of triangle

S = circle at the top of the diagonal edge of the triangle.

TS = right-angled corner to the left, long edge at the bottom with the circle at the top of the diagonal edge of the triangle.

6. **E**

Both pictures starting **L** have a total number of 12 sides to the shapes so the first letter must be the total number of sides:

L = 12 sides

W = nine sides

Z = eight sides

F = 11 sides.

Both pictures ending **M** have vertical stripes in some of the shapes so the last letter must be the direction of the stripes:

M = vertical stripes

A = diagonal stripes

N = horizontal stripes.

WN = nine sides in total with horizontal stripes.

Page 62 1. **D**

Both pictures starting **F** have three stars so the first letter must be the number of stars:

F = three stars

T = two stars

Y = one star.

Both pictures ending **J** have a diagonal arrow pointing down to the right, so the second letter must be the direction of the arrow:

J = arrow pointing diagonally down to the right

P = arrow pointing diagonally down to the left

D = arrow pointing vertically down.

TD = two stars and arrow pointing vertically down.

2. **B**

Both pictures starting **S** have a large oval on the outside of the image so the first letter must be the outer shape:

S = large oval

W = large rectangle

L = large square.

Both pictures ending **H** have a small black square in the centre so the second letter must describe the central shape:

H = small black square

V = small white rectangle

A = small grey oval.

LV = large outer square and small white rectangle in the centre.

3. **C**

   Both pictures starting **G** are large squares so the first letter must describe the shape:

   G = square **U** = triangle
   Z = rectangle.

   Both pictures ending **K** have a quarter of the shape shaded black so the last letter must describe the fraction of the shape that is shaded black:

   K = $\frac{1}{4}$ **N** = $\frac{1}{2}$
   R = $\frac{1}{9}$.

   UN = large triangle of which half is shaded black.

4. **D**

   Both pictures starting **B** have black arrows and both pictures starting **P** have white arrows so the first letter must describe the colour of the arrow:

   B = black **P** = white
   Q = grey.

   Both pictures ending **L** have four lines crossing the arrow so the second letter must describe the number of lines:

   L = four lines **E** = three lines
   T = one line **F** = two lines.

   QF = grey arrow with two lines.

5. **A**

   Both pictures starting **H** have horizontal arrows curving down and pointing right so the first letter must describe the arrow direction:

   H = horizontal arrow curving down and pointing right **Z** = vertical arrow curving right and pointing up
   D = horizontal arrow curving down and pointing left **K** = horizontal arrow curving up and pointing right.

   Both pictures ending **W** are grey so the second letter must describe colour:

   W = grey **Y** = diagonal stripes
   V = black with white spots **M** = white with black spots.

   ZY = vertical arrow curving right and pointing up with diagonal stripes.

6. **B**

   Both pictures starting **S** have horizontal stripes so the first letter must be the type of shading:

   S = horizontal stripes **E** = white with black spots
   C = criss cross pattern **P** = black.

   Both pictures ending **X** have a line across the shape and both ending **G** have a single-headed arrow so the second letter must describe the type of line:

   X = line **L** = double-headed arrow
   G = single-headed arrow.

   CL = criss cross pattern with a double-headed arrow.

Page 63 1. E

Both pictures starting **F** have a large black triangle so the first letter must describe the large black shape:

F = large black triangle   **S** = large black rectangle
Z = large black oval   **V** = large black trapezium.

Both pictures ending **N** have a vertical line to the right of the large black shape, so the second letter must describe the position of the line:

N = vertical to the right   **U** = horizontal to the top
B = vertical to the left   **D** = horizontal to the bottom.

ZU = large black oval with horizontal line to the top.

2. C

Both pictures starting **Y** have five circles and both starting **H** have four circles so the first letter must describe the number of circles:

Y = five circles   **H** = four circles
P = three circles.

Both pictures ending **R** have one black circle and both ending **M** have three black circles so the second letter must describe the number of black circles:

R = one black circle   **G** = two black circles
M = three black circles.

PG = three circles, two of which are black.

3. A

Both pictures starting **G** have horizontal arrows pointing to the right so the first letter must describe the position of the arrow:

G = horizontal arrow pointing right   **D** = vertical arrow pointing up
A = vertical arrow pointing down   **X** = horizontal arrow pointing left.

Both pictures ending **L** have two squares and both ending **B** have three squares so the second letter must describe the number of squares:

L = two squares   **B** = three squares
V = one square.

DL = vertical arrow pointing up with two squares.

4. B

Both pictures starting **W** have a black rectangle and both starting **Q** have a white rectangle so the first letter must describe the colour of the rectangle:

W = black rectangle   **J** = grey rectangle
Q = white rectangle.

Both pictures ending **E** have three arrow heads so the second letter must be describing the number of arrow heads:

E = three arrow heads   **K** = two arrow heads
C = five arrow heads   **U** = one arrow head.

JU = grey rectangle with one arrow head.

5. E

Both pictures starting **L** have a jointed line made up of six lines so the first letter must describe the number of lines within the jointed line:

L = six lines   **T** = five lines
P = three lines   **B** = four lines.

Both pictures ending **F** have two triangles and both ending **H** have one triangle so the second letter must describe the number of triangles:

F = two triangles   **H** = one triangle
C = three triangles.

TF = five lines in the jointed line and two triangles.

6. B

Both pictures starting **V** have a horizontal line so the first letter must describe the line:

V = horizontal   **M** = vertical
K = diagonal from top left to   **Z** = diagonal from top right to
      bottom right   bottom left.

In both pictures ending **G** the number of sides on the shapes is 12 so the second letter must describe the number of sides:

G = 12 sides   **J** = 11 sides
X = 15 sides   **D** = 10 sides.

MJ = vertical line with a total of 11 sides.

Page 65 1. a) First shape:

A – The outer circle has changed from white to black and the inner circle has changed from black to white.
B – The square has been stretched into a rectangle.
C – Stayed the same.
D – Stayed the same.
E – Stayed the same.
The shape has stayed the same in images **C**, **D** and **E**.

b) Second shape:

A – Same shape, rotated 90°.
B – Same shape.
C – An extra perpendicular line has been added to cross the long central line.
D – Same shape, rotated 90°.
E – The central line is shorter.
The shape has stayed the same in images **A**, **B** and **D**.

Answer: **D**. In both cases the shapes stayed the same.

Page 66 1. C

First shape	Second shape
A – Only one black circle.	**A** – Same shape.
B – Same shape, hidden behind the second shape.	**B** – Line not visible through the centre of the circle.

Answers

C – Same shape, hidden behind the second shape.

D – White circle on the wrong side of the square.

E – Same shape.

C – Same shape.

D – Same shape.

E – Line too short.

2. E

First shape

A – Lines at top and bottom too long.

B – Line at bottom too short.

C – Same shape, rotated 180°.

D – Same shape.

E – Same shape, rotated 90° clockwise.

Second shape

A – Same shape.

B – Same shape.

C – Missing horizontal line through the middle.

D – Too large.

E – Same shape, rotated 90°.

3. B

First shape

A – Only two vertical lines instead of three.

B – Same shape.

C – Same shape.

D – Arrow is white not black.

E – Same shape.

Second shape

A – Same shape.

B – Same shape, rotated 90° clockwise.

C – The shape has been reflected in a vertical mirror line.

D – Same shape.

E – The shape has been reflected in a horizontal mirror line.

4. A

First shape

A – Same shape.

B – Same shape, rotated 90°.

C – The cross in the circle has rotated but the rest of the shape has not.

D – The top diagonal lines are too short.

E – Same shape.

Second shape

A – Same shape.

B – The semi-circle has turned from black to white.

C – Same shape.

D – Same shape, rotated 90° anticlockwise.

E – Missing a diagonal line.

5. E

First shape

A – Too long.

B – Too fat.

C – Same shape.

D – Missing the rectangle down the centre.

E – Same shape.

Second shape

A – Same shape.

B – Same shape.

C – Line too short.

D – Same shape.

E – Same shape.

6. C

First shape

A – Black rectangle has become white.

Second shape

A – Same shape.

Answers

B – Same shape, rotated 90° anticlockwise.
C – Same shape.
D – White circle has become black.
E – Black rectangle has become white and white circle has become black.

B – Line too long.
C – Same shape.
D – Same shape.
E – The white circles have turned black.

Page 67 **1. E**

First shape
A – Same shape.

B – Same shape.
C – Same shape.
D – There is no vertical line in the oval.
E – Same shape.

Second shape
A – No arrow heads on the horizontal line.
B – No arrow heads at all.
C – No horizontal arrows.
D – Same shape.
E – Same shape.

2. B

First shape
A – Has been reflected in a vertical mirror line.
B – Same shape, rotated 90° clockwise.
C – Has been reflected in a horizontal mirror line.
D – Same shape.
E – Same shape.

Second shape
A – Same shape.

B – Same shape.

C – Same shape, rotated 180°.

D – There is no vertical line.
E – The line has moved to the left end of the rectangle.

3. D

First shape
A – Has been reflected in a vertical mirror line.
B – Has been reflected in a horizontal mirror line.
C – Same shape, rotated 90° clockwise.
D – Same shape.
E – Has been reflected in a vertical mirror line and then rotated 90° clockwise.

Second shape
A – Same shape.

B – Same shape, rotated 180°.

C – The white triangle is much smaller.
D – Same shape.
E – Same shape.

4. A

First shape
A – Same shape.
B – Shape has been reflected in a vertical mirror line.
C – Same shape, rotated 90°.

Second shape
A – Same shape.
B – Same shape.

C – The black and white circles have swapped colours.

D – Has been reflected in a horizontal mirror line and then rotated 90° anticlockwise.

E – Has been reflected in a vertical mirror line.

D – Same shape.

E – Same shape.

5. E

First shape

A – Has been reflected in a vertical mirror line.

B – The bottom arrow has come in front of the main shape having been rotated 90° anticlockwise.

C – Same shape.

D – Has been reflected in a vertical mirror line.

E – Same shape.

Second shape

A – Same shape.

B – Same shape, rotated 90° clockwise.

C – Has been reflected in a vertical mirror line.

D – Same shape.

E – Same shape.

6. B

First shape

A – Same shape.

B – Same shape.

C – Has been reflected in a vertical mirror line.

D – Has been reflected in a vertical mirror line.

E – Same shape, rotated 90°.

Second shape

A – Has been reflected in a vertical mirror line.

B – Same shape.

C – Same shape, rotated 90° clockwise.

D – Same shape.

E – Has been reflected in a vertical mirror line.

age 68 1. B

First shape

A – The white rectangle has moved to the other side of the line.

B – Same shape, rotated 90° anticlockwise.

C – Same shape.

D – The black rectangle has turned white.

E – Same shape, rotated 90° clockwise.

Second shape

A – Same shape.

B – Same shape, rotated 90° anticlockwise.

C – The line has disappeared inside the rectangle.

D – Same shape.

E – The small rectangle has moved.

2. E

First shape

A – The dotted line has disappeared.

B – The dashes on the lines are too small.

Second shape

A – Same shape.

B – Same shape.

C – The black circle has become white.

D – The black circle is too big.

E – Same shape.

3. A

First shape
A – Same shape, rotated 180°.
B – The rectangle is not touching the triangle.
C – Same shape.
D – Same shape, rotated 90° anticlockwise.
E – Same shape.

4. B

First shape
A – The black rectangle has moved nearer the triangle.
B – Same shape, rotated 180°.
C – The black rectangle has become white.
D – The triangle has changed position.

E – Same shape.

5. C

First shape
A – The rectangle with the star in is no longer touching the shaded rectangle.
B – Same shape.

C – Same shape.
D – The star has become white.
E – The shading of the rectangle has changed.

6. D

First shape
A – Has been reflected in a vertical mirror line.
B – Same shape.
C – Same shape, rotated 90°.

C – The black ring has become white and the centre has become black.

D – The black ring has become white and the centre has become black.

E – Same shape.

Second shape
A – Same shape, rotated 180°.
B – Same shape, rotated 90° clockwise.
C – The end rectangles are too low.
D – The two small rectangles are the wrong side of the line.
E – The two small rectangles are missing

Second shape
A – Same shape, rotated 90° clockwise.
B – Same shape, rotated 90° clockwise.
C – Same shape.

D – Same shape, rotated 90° anticlockwise.
E – The rectangle has become much wider.

Second shape
A – Same shape, rotated 90° clockwise.

B – The parallelogram is incorrectly positioned within the larger rectangle.
C – Same shape, rotated 180°.
D – Same shape.
E – Same shape, rotated 90° anticlockwise.

Second shape
A – Has been reflected in a horizontal mirror line.
B – The vertical line has moved.
C – The size of the lines has changed.

D – Same shape, rotated 90°.

E – The size of the jointed line has changed.

D – Same shape, rotated 90° anticlockwise.

E – Same shape.

age 69 **1. A**

First shape

A – Same shape, rotated 180°.
B – The line in the square has disappeared.
C – Same shape.
D – The line to the triangle is too long.
E – The square is missing.

Second shape

A – Same shape, rotated 180°.
B – Same shape.

C – There is no black circle.
D – Same shape.
E – Same shape, rotated 180°.

2. B

First shape

A – Same shape, rotated 90° clockwise

B – Same shape.

C – The line has gone behind the rectangle.
D – The arrow line is too long.
E – Same shape.

Second shape

A – The point of the triangle is no longer facing the circle.
B – Same shape, rotated 90° anticlockwise.
C – Same shape.

D – Same shape.
E – Too big.

3. C

First shape

A – The rectangle is too big.
B – Same shape.
C – Same shape, rotated 90° clockwise.
D – Same shape, rotated 90° anticlockwise.
E – Has been reflected in a horizontal mirror line.

Second shape

A – Same shape, rotated 90° clockwise.
B – Too small.
C – Same shape, rotated 90° clockwise.
D – Too big.
E – Same shape.

4. D

First shape

A – Same shape, rotated 90° clockwise.

B – A line is missing.

C – The top horizontal line has been moved down.
D – Same shape, rotated 90° clockwise.
E – Same shape, rotated 90° anticlockwise.

Second shape

A – The black rectangle has become white.
B – Same shape, rotated 90° anticlockwise.
C – Same shape.

D – Same shape, rotated 90° clockwise.
E – The black rectangle is too high up the arrow.

5. A

First shape

A – Same shape, rotated 90° clockwise.

B – Same shape.

C – Same shape, rotated 90° anticlockwise.

D – Has been reflected in a horizontal mirror line.

E – Same shape, rotated 180°.

Second shape

A – Same shape.

B – The two vertical triangles have swapped places.

C – Has been reflected in a horizontal mirror line.

D – Same shape, rotated 90° clockwise.

E – The horizontal triangle has moved on rotation.

6. A

First shape

A – Same shape, rotated 90° clockwise.

B – The smaller jointed arrow has moved further down.

C – Same shape.

D – An extra arrow has been added.

E – Has been reflected in a vertical mirror line.

Second shape

A – Same shape, rotated 90° anticlockwise.

B – Same shape.

C – The horizontal line has moved on rotation.

D – Has been reflected in a horizontal mirror line.

E – Same shape.

Tips for tests

These tips will be useful as you prepare for school tests, such as the 11+, and for practice tests that you do at school or at home.

- Always read the questions carefully.

- In multiple choice tests, don't just choose the first answer you see that you think is right. Check every answer option to make sure you have definitely picked the right one.

- Mark your answer clearly and make sure you know what to do if you make a mistake. In some tests you are asked to rub out an incorrect answer. In others you are asked to cross it out.

- Don't spend too long on one question. If you are finding it difficult, put a circle around the question number and then come back to it at the end if you have time. By putting a circle around the number you'll be able to see easily which ones you need to go back to.

- If you finish before the end, **go back and check your answers**, especially any you weren't completely sure about. You'd be surprised how many people make silly mistakes or even leave out whole pages of questions by mistake.

- If there is a question you really can't answer, you might as well have a guess. With multiple choice answers, it is worth a try. You never know, you might guess the right answer.

- When you are doing a practice test, ask an adult to time you and let you know when you are half way through the test – and when you have five minutes left. This will help you to become more aware of how quickly you need to work.

- In most non-verbal reasoning question types, similar methods are used to answer the questions. Remember to look out for these eight features:
  - colour
  - shape
  - direction
  - reflection
  - size
  - position
  - rotation
  - number of sides/lines/shapes.

Tips for revision

- Practice is the key. The more you do, the better you will get.

- When revising for a test, give more time to practising the question types you are weaker in as this will help you to improve.

- Since timing is important for tests, develop your sense of time by asking an adult to time you while you attempt fun challenges, such as 'How many times can I write my name in one minute?' or 'How many jumps can I do in 30 seconds?'

- Make sure that you have a quiet place in which to work, without any distractions.

A good way to help develop your non-verbal reasoning skills is to play 'observational' games. These are games in which you have to look carefully at things, such as 'Spot the Difference' and 'Kim's Game'. Games like these may help you to become more observant.

Index and glossary

alternate 51	happening in turns – first one, then the other – or next but one
analogy 17 (pl. **analogies** 17–23)	a way of comparing similar things
anticlockwise 18	moving round in a circle in the opposite direction to the hands on a clock
clockwise 18, 39	moving round in a circle in the same direction as the hands on a clock
code 58–63	a set of signs, letters or numbers with a hidden meaning
column 37	a **vertical** line of items, running from top to bottom
combined 64–69	two or more things that are joined together as one
common to 12	having some of the same features as
cube 51–57	a 3-D shape with six square faces
diagonal 25, 46	not **horizontal** or **vertical** but sloped, like a line that would join the opposite two corners of a rectangle
difference 6, 11, 12, 17, 26, 31, 39	the feature that makes something unlike something else, so that the two are not the same
hidden 31–36	in a place where it may not easily be seen or found
horizontal 19, 44, 46, 51	going across from left to right or right to left so that it is level, like the line where the sky appears to meet the land or the sea (which is called the horizon)
image 19, 44, 64, 65	what you see, whether it is a picture, something that you see through a lens, or a **reflection**
in common 4, 6–10, 11, 12, 18, 58, 59	having some of the same features
logic 2	a way of thinking in which, step by step, you use each fact that you already know to find out other facts that are less obvious
matrix 37, 39 (pl. **matrices** 37–43)	a set of images, letters or numbers arranged in a grid or table, with **rows** and **columns**
net 51–57	a flattened 2-D outline of a 3-D shape
odd one out 11–16	the one that is different from all the others
overlap 64	where something extends over and across onto something else
perpendicular 4, 5	at **right angles**
reflect(ed) 19, 38, 39, 44–50, 64	to provide an **image** of an object (for example, a mirror, a piece of glass and the water in a still pool are all able to provide reflected images, also known as reflections)
right angle 18, 31	an angle of 90°, like the angles that you find in a square or rectangle
rotate(d) 18, 19, 32, 39, 44, 53, 64, 65	to turn around a fixed point; an **image** that has been rotated may sometimes be referred to as a rotation
row 37	a **horizontal** line of items, running from left to right or right to left
sequence 24, 37, 38	the special order in which a particular set or **series** of items (for example, pictures, objects, letters or numbers) is arranged
series 24, 26–30, 37	a set of items (for example, pictures, objects, letters or numbers) arranged in a special order or **sequence**
similarity 4, 12 (pl. **similarities** 4–12, 17, 26, 31)	a feature or quality that is shared by two or more different things, making them almost the same but not quite
symmetry 44 (adj. **symmetrical**)	when the parts of an object or **image** are exactly the same on either side of a real or imaginary straight line drawn down the centre
vertical 19, 46, 51	going directly up or down, like a tree trunk, at **right angles** to something **horizontal** – such as the horizon or the floor